Richard Sylvester is a humanistic psychologist, therapist and lecturer. For thirty years he engaged with a variety of spiritual practices while also training in psychotherapeutic techniques and teaching counselling. In 2002 Richard met Tony Parsons and, as he writes in his first book, *I Hope You Die Soon*, "That was the end of what I thought had been my life". There then occurred two events which he describes in his book as 'awakening' and 'liberation'. Richard lives in a country town in South East England. He holds meetings about non-duality in London and other locations in the U.K.

Readers' Comments on 'I Hope You Die Soon' by Richard Sylvester

I have just finished reading your book 'I Hope You Die Soon'. I want to thank you. It is totally releasing. And I had so much fun and laughter reading it. *R.G. – Germany*

Sometimes I come across a book which conveys the sharing of Oneness in a very simple direct way. Your book fell into my hands a few weeks ago. It would be an injustice not to e-mail you to thank you for the sharing of this seeing. It's so direct and without any spiritual romanticism. It leaves nothing to be played with. A BIG thanks to you for this sharing. *A.M. – U.K.*

Thank you for making the impossible possible! Thank you for having written this book! Now, it finally makes sense that nothing ever made sense! *B.S. – Switzerland*

I have read your book many times. It is perhaps the most direct and helpful expression and description of what awakening and liberation are and are not that I have read in over thirty years of reading. *I.M. – France*

I have been reading your book and I have to tell you I have been laughing so much! It's all about me, that book. *M.F. – Canada*

I really enjoyed your book – clear words that opened up awareness behind the words – thank you. *M.S. – U.K.*

The words in your book are such sweet perfume. *D.H. – U.S.A.*

I want to thank you most gratefully for your wonderful book. I immediately knew the book was for me by its title. I simply love it and your sense of humour and its simplicity. Although I have long finished the book, I carry it off to bed with me every night and read a page or two before going to sleep. *E.D. – U.K.*

Just read your book.... it's great.... thanks. What can be said? There is a sense of gratitude for this book and what appears to happen is this e-mail communicating about this gratitude. *C.B. – Holland*

Last night I read your book 'I Hope You Die Soon', in German 'Erleuchtet – und was jetzt'. Thank you so much for these words, although I know words cannot describe This. I read it and all I can say is "Yes, yes, it is That. *J.B. – Germany*

I have just finished your book over the weekend and I found it a delightful read. Everything you stated resonated with me strongly as true. *D.C. – U.K.*

I'm writing for my husband and myself to thank you for your book 'I Hope You Die Soon'. While we understand that Oneness wrote it and Oneness read it, in this physicality the pointing to was a good read. We too have sought the final enlightenment through various disciplines. What a relief to find there is nowhere to go, nothing to do and nothing to be accomplished. Unconditional love is all there is. Isn't that fantastic? *J.S. – U.S.A.*

Yesterday I read your book and was very touched by it. It felt as if they were my own words. It expressed so well what I would like to say about how it is, but I cannot find the words to express it. So thank you very much. *R.R. – Holland*

Also by Richard Sylvester

I Hope You Die Soon – Words on Non-duality
and Liberation

The Book of No One

Talks And Dialogues on Non-duality and Liberation

by **Richard Sylvester**

NON-DUALITY PRESS
UNITED KINGDOM

With deep appreciation to Tony Parsons for communicating
non-duality so clearly and with such love and humour.

First published April 2008 by Non-Duality Press

Typeset in Warnock Pro 11/13

Non-Duality Press, Salisbury, SP2 8JP
United Kingdom.

ISBN 978-0-9558290-2-4

www.non-dualitybooks.com

"Now tell me what Nirvana is."

"Here... You are there already. You are in Nirvana. You are like a fish claiming it is thirsty. You are right in the middle of it. Here. Here."

Janwillem van de Wetering
A Glimpse Of Nothingness

Contents

Introduction

There are several conflicting views on consciousness. For example, among scientists the most popular view is that consciousness is an accidental by-product of matter. Many scientists hold that as matter, the physical stuff of the universe, becomes more and more complex in evolving brains, consciousness emerges, as it were by chance. When the brain dies, consciousness ends. Some people find this a depressing view. Others, perhaps more surprisingly, are relieved by this thought. In a book about euthanasia called 'Dancing With Mr. D' by Bert Keizer, an old lady reprimands a smarmy young man, who is trying to sell her a system for recording her memories for her descendants, with the words "Young man, you'll find that at my age nothing matters."

Many religious people on the other hand hold that consciousness is separate from matter and resides in the soul. The soul is considered to be primary and the world of matter is often thought to be a kind of school where the soul is tested or put through its paces or given the opportunity to learn certain lessons. Depending on the precise nature of the religion, if the soul does well it may either be united with God or earn a favourable rebirth.

The spiritual view of the connection between consciousness and matter is more complex. The physical universe is sometimes thought of as an emanation of consciousness and the particular nature of the world the person lives in may be seen as a creation of their individual psyche. So if we want to change the nature of our external reality, we must cultivate self-responsibility and change our internal reality. Other spiritual outlooks stress instead that as it is the nature of external reality always to be transitory, as everything is constantly subject to change, it is wiser to cultivate acceptance.

In this book I have presented another view, that consciousness is not only primary but it is all that there is, that the appearance of ourselves and of the world we live in is consciousness appearing as everything. The waves and the foam are not separate from the ocean that gives rise to them and we are not separate from the light of consciousness in which we and everything else arise. Even though this may not be understood by the mind, it may be seen in liberation. Then it may be known that there is no self and that "Everything that comes from birth undoes itself in liberation."

Richard Sylvester
April, 2008

1

Some Preliminaries

*You have said that seeing non-duality is the end of meaning
and the end of purpose. Would you say that duality has
meaning and purpose?*

It appears to. For as long as there is the sense of a separate person,
the world of duality is taken to be utterly real and probably highly
meaningful and very purposive. The mind has a powerful urge to
search for meaning. But when it is seen that there was never any
person, this is seen as a dream and it is seen as without purpose.
In the same way, when we wake up from a night-time dream, it is
obvious that it is without purpose, although the mind may very
well be tempted to add a meaning to it later on by interpreting it.

Is there a purpose in non-duality manifesting as duality?

We pretend that we've lost paradise only for the joy of finding it
again. When paradise is regained, it's realised that it was never
lost.

But as long as we're searching for paradise, it is impossible to notice that this is already it.

Is there a higher purpose?

As soon as we start talking about higher and lower purpose we are back in the story of duality. There is no higher or lower. There is only this.

We as human beings invented the search for a higher purpose?

You as a human being are a dream character. A dream character cannot invent anything.

When Oneness stops dreaming of duality, does the physical world disappear?

The dream ends at death. Death is liberation from the dream.

I think death is just another dream, another illusion.

You are right. What the person thinks of as death is an illusion.

I think if the person believes they'll get an after-life, they will. If they don't, they won't. If they believe in an after-life, they'll get whatever they believe in.

That's a cute story.

In the bible story, we're in the Garden of Eden and then we gain self-knowledge and we lose that situation.

Yes, self-knowledge gives rise to separation and the loss of the sense of paradise.

So in the biblical metaphor it seems possible that awareness is still intact over here and we are projections outside of that, an illusion that has arisen in order for awareness to know what it's not. It can't know what it is unless it knows what it's not. The purpose of a dream is to act as a metaphor for experiences that have happened to us.

A dream has no purpose but the mind will create one. We only have to look at the shelves of psychology books to see that the mind will create a dozen different purposes for dreams.

There is nothing that awareness is not. 'Everything' is awareness arising as everything.

The danger in this theory, in saying that there is no purpose, is that you're arguing that nothing matters, not if we start a war, not if we drop a nuclear bomb. I can't accept that.

I'm not arguing anything. I'm just trying to describe something. And I'm suggesting that there is nobody who can start a war or drop a nuclear bomb. What happens in the drama simply happens.

I can't accept that it doesn't matter if I go out and murder someone.

I'm not saying that it doesn't matter if you go out and murder somebody. I'm saying that there is no 'you' who can choose to do that. Murdering people does sometimes happen in the drama, but unless there's the character of a murderer sitting there, it's very unlikely that you will go out and murder someone.

What happens is simply what happens. So you don't need to worry that you are going to unleash the hounds of hell on the high street.

There is no volition at any level. So you can't hear these words and then, as a result of them, choose to go out and murder someone. Or rob a bank.

But that's clearly not the case, because I can.

As long as there's the sense of a person, there will be the feeling that you can choose to act. This is an appearance which drops away when it is seen that there is only Oneness. Then it's seen that the person always was the divine puppet. What is sitting there, although it might feel itself to be a person, is the light in which everything arises.

Is there no morality?

No.

Then there's anarchy and I can murder somebody.

This is what a person says. "If there's no morality, I can do whatever I like." But that is not what I am saying. I am saying that there is no morality because there is no person who can choose to do anything. Therefore *you* can't do what you like.

I'm not saying "You can make choices, but there's no morality so it doesn't matter what choices you make." I'm saying phenomena arise, and it may be noticed that no one is causing them, no one is choosing them.

Looking at you, I'd say that the phenomenon of you murdering someone is rather unlikely to arise.

It could be you. You're getting quite close. (Laughter)

(Laughing) Yes, if it's going to be anyone in here, I'm getting the impression that it will be me. Nevertheless, looking at the psychophysical organism sitting there, I still think you're most unlikely to have the character of a murderer. But I could be wrong.

✳✳✳✳✳✳✳✳✳

Is awareness the mind?

No. The mind is just a series of thoughts arising in awareness. For example, a memory that I drove here today is just a thought

4

arising in this. If you look for the one who thinks these thoughts, you will never find them.

Is there nothing that we can cling on to?

No. There's nothing to cling on to. We're in a hopeless case here. As far as the mind is concerned, everything is stripped away.

What about the thought that there's nobody here?

That's just another thought. When the person drops away, it's seen that the self is empty and there is simply this. That is not a thought.

Paradoxically, when the self is seen to be empty, this is seen to be full. Then there is nothing left to search for.

If there's no choice, why is there a preference for some things over others?

A preference is just a preference. A character tends to have preferences – for tea rather than for coffee, for example. Where there's the sense of a person, that preference may attach itself to the feeling that I am making a choice about it. But there's no such choice being made because there's no one to make it.

If the person preferred tea before liberation was seen, it's probable that the character will go on preferring tea afterwards.

But for some people, particularly those with a more ascetic nature, there's something very attractive about not having preferences. It's associated with an ideal of detached holiness and in some spiritual paths there is a very powerful notion that we should be able to identify an enlightened one partly by their lack of preferences. They may be thought to live in a state of bliss in which it doesn't matter whether they get tea or coffee, or pain or pleasure. This state of detachment has no connection with liberation but it can seem extremely attractive to us if we are spiritual seekers. And very importantly, it can confirm our own sense of inadequacy, which it is necessary for us to maintain if we are to continue seeking. It may matter a lot to us whether we get tea or coffee, particularly if we are in an uncomfortable ashram half way up a Himalaya. Our strong desire for our morning cuppa may confirm that we are miserable worms still enmeshed in samsara, compared to our beloved guru who seems to have risen above all such worldly concerns.

A seeker who is looking for a spiritual master to idealise and follow, may find a teacher who idealises themselves as a spiritual master and is looking for seekers who will follow them . It's a marriage made in heaven. It's a beautiful symbiotic relationship. My sinfulness can be washed away by your spiritual light. You can be sustained in your view of yourself by my wishing to be your devoted follower.

****

I've read that for some people, awakening has been accompanied by or followed by a lot of fear. Is that because they haven't prepared themselves, by meditating for example?

No. Sometimes liberation may be seen by someone who has never even heard of the word with no fear accompanying it or following it at all.

But regardless of what we've done, someone may be in a state of 'right-mindedness' or 'preparedness'. Does our state of mind affect how long it takes for us to see this or what happens when we do?

No. There's no such thing as 'right-mindedness' or 'preparedness' and there's no cause and effect. In the story, alcoholism may apparently precede liberation or meditation may.

****

You seem to have quite a lot of insight into this.

I don't have anything. If there's insight here, it isn't mine. It's just what's arising. Insight may arise. A cup of tea may arise. So what?

Some people hear that "So what?" as if it's nihilistic or despairing or dismissive. But paradoxically, it's only when that "So what?" arises that this can be seen to be already paradise. When that "So what?" arises, there's no need to look for miracles, because this is already seen to be a miracle.

The description that there is only emptiness can also be heard as nihilistic. People often want to argue with this on a philosophical level. When they do, they commonly make two accusations against it, that it is nihilistic and solipsistic. But it isn't either of these. And it isn't a philosophical standpoint, it's a description.

People accuse this of being nihilistic because they hear it as saying "There is no morality, there are no values, so we might just as well go out onto the streets and start murdering people to our hearts' content."

They accuse this of being solipsistic because solipsism is the philosophy that only I exist. According to solipsism, you are just an apparition in my consciousness. I hope it's obvious by now that this isn't solipsistic. Firstly, it isn't a philosophy and secondly, it doesn't hold that only I exist. It holds the opposite. It holds that I don't exist.

On a conceptual level, this is sometimes misunderstood in these two ways. But you have to tie yourself into considerable knots to hear "There is no one" as "I am the only one who exists." That's quite a leap. It's also quite a leap to hear "There is no one" as "I can go out and murder people with impunity" but this accusation is made surprisingly often.

If this is all there is, when we leave here will the street appear?

That's my bet. *(Laughter)*

What happens when we go to sleep?

The person is disassembled. Then there's either dreaming or there's nothing. But the nothing isn't necessarily an empty nothing.

In the morning the person wakes up and is reassembled.

Are you aware in dreamless sleep?

I'm not. There is awareness.

The night-time dream seems much less consistent than the day-time dream.

Yes, that's why the day-time dream is so addictive. Night-time dreams are very inconsistent so they're quite easy to see through, but the day-time dream has so much consistency that it is very difficult to see through.

****

Are human beings the only species that is self-aware?

Human beings are uniquely self-aware. A cat may feel fear but it doesn't think "If I went to a therapist and dealt with my fear issues, I'd be a more fulfilled cat."

****

Whether you want to call this something or nothing, we're here for a reason. Perhaps we could approach it in a scientific, methodical way.

We could if we were here and if there was a reason. But there's no here, there's no we and there's no reason. This is simply what is.

Some people get excited by the connections they see between non-duality and certain scientific discoveries, particularly in quantum physics. In some ways quantum physics gives descriptions of existence which sound similar to this. But they are only metaphors. No language or thought can be more than a metaphorical description of this.

The human species has a built-in drive not just to survive but to be self-determined. Do you think it's worthwhile trying to bring about an improvement in conditions for humanity?

Who would do that? An improvement in conditions for people may or may not happen but there's no one who can bring that about. In the story, it's clear that sometimes conditions improve and sometimes they deteriorate.

Why can't we wake ourselves up?

The person who embarks on a spiritual path is, it appears, trying to wake up. It's impossible for them to see that the person who is trying to wake up is a false person.

I'm trying to relate this to my personal experience.

You can't. Because there's no you and this is not about a personal experience.

Why did you write a book about this?

I didn't write a book. Books get written. But if you want a biographical answer, this character has always been a communicator. I've been a professional lecturer for many years. For another character, when this is seen there might be no impulse to communicate about it in any way.

Is there any reason why we can't see the truth of this even when we're seeking for it?

If that character sitting there has an impulse to seek for truth, it will probably do that. But as far as I'm concerned, what we're talking about here has nothing to do with truth. Firstly, truth is about concepts and secondly, truth isn't an absolute. There are many different versions of truth. What is being attempted here is a description of the indescribable. That's got nothing to do with truth. It makes no more sense to say that what is being said here is true than to say that a flower is true. Or to ponder about the true feelings that the hero of a film has. He doesn't have any feelings because he doesn't exist.

There used to be a fashion in literary criticism for speculating about the past and the future of fictional characters and about their life beyond the work of art in which they appear. A critic called L.C. Knights wrote a very good book to try to put an end to this. It was called 'How Many Children Had Lady Macbeth?' because we know from a reference in the play that Lady Macbeth had children but we're not told how many:

> 'I have given suck, and know
> How tender 'tis to love the babe that milks me.'

Various scholarly minds might exercise themselves trying to work out how many children she had, or what subject Hamlet was studying at university before he was summoned home to the funeral of his father. L.C. Knights points out that this is absurd. Fictional characters have no past or future or life beyond the page because they do not exist.

You and I are fictional characters.

The journey that you think you took to arrive here – the car you drove, the route you took, the road you parked in – has no more reality than the journey that Rick took by train in 'Casablanca' to escape from the invasion of Paris.

All there is, is this. This may include the thought that I made a car journey here today. That's just a thought.

✴✴✴✴✴✴✴✴✴

How can we be certain that we have found the truth?

There is no truth. Certainty is often a highly dangerous mindset. Those who have found certainty have a tendency to slaughter the heathens, knowing that they will be rewarded in paradise with seventy-two virgins.

I've heard they've reduced the number. (Laughter)

That's the trouble with modern morality. You can't get the virgins anymore.

I would be highly suspicious of certainty. Certainty is about beliefs, creeds, and philosophies. "We will have paradise when we've created the socialist revolution" or "We will have paradise when we've slaughtered the infidels."

I would avoid people who have certainty like the plague.

****

When did it all begin?

There is no beginning. This is the eternal play.

What about the Big Bang?

The Big Bang is an idea, it's a thought which is manifesting in this. There's nowhere else for it to manifest.

Is there really nothing else but this?

If there were anything else but this, it would still be this. "All there is, is this" is an absolute brick wall. The mind cannot get beyond it – or batter its way through it. This encompasses whatever phenomena arise. If there were anything beyond non-duality it would still be non-duality. Wittgenstein accidentally got very close to expressing this when he wrote "The world is everything that is the case."

****

Several teachers recommend focussing on the present moment, noticing what's going on right now, whatever's happening in our immediate attention. Just listen to the traffic, be aware of sensations, be in the now.

11

Who's going to do that? Listening to the traffic happens or it does not. Being in the now happens or it does not.

On a psychological level, noticing what's happening in presence can be helpful to a person. But it doesn't have anything to do with liberation and there's no one who can create doing that or who can choose to do that. There's nothing wrong with a teacher suggesting that you can choose to 'be in the now' and that this has something to do with liberation, but it happens to be highly misleading.

I've read people who say almost exactly the same as this but there's a suggestion that non-duality is what ultimately offers relief from suffering.

So the message is "Come to non-duality and you will be saved, Brothers and Sisters"?

I suppose so, yes.

Personal suffering can be relieved while we are engaged with non-duality. But it can also be relieved while we're sitting on a bus reading a newspaper or drinking lager in a bar.

I've heard it suggested that if a serious enquiry is made under the right guidance for two weeks, there can be breakthroughs, transformation and insight.

There may be all of these but none of them have anything to do with liberation, except that they all arise within liberation, as does everything else. Spiritual techniques, particularly if they're practised regularly over long periods of time, can produce many breakthroughs, much transformation and a good few insights. Then we have a transformed, insightful person who has experienced breakthroughs. The person will probably feel that every breakthrough, each transformation and every insight is intimately connected with liberation. It can't be seen until the person drops away that none of these have anything to do with it.

If a person believes in relieving their suffering through materialism they might want a better car. If they believe in relieving their suffering through spiritual means, they might want a better mantra. It's very difficult for the person not to want these things because ever since they first had self-consciousness, the evidence supports their belief that they will feel better, at least for a little while, if they get the things that they want. It's only when the person falls away that it's seen that liberation cannot possibly have anything to do with 'me' or with anything I thought I was doing.

The whole idea that I can get somewhere by Being Here Now, clearing my chakras or meditating arises out of a sense of personal inadequacy and the thought that I can do something to make myself more adequate. This is why there is sometimes a lot of laughter when the person drops away. It's suddenly seen what a joke it is that there never was anybody who was inadequate or who needed improving. There is only divinity. How can divinity be improved?

Is there a connection between being interested in this, coming to meetings like this, and coming to the point of awakening?

There is no choice about whether an interest in this arises or not, so it doesn't matter.

There's no cause and effect. Liberation is an uncaused spontaneous arising. So is this glass of water. Everything is an uncaused spontaneous arising. But the mind always has to think in terms of cause and effect. It's natural for it to do so. The mind has to be in control and it can't give up control of its own volition. When the mind says "I'm giving up control now", it's controlling giving up control.

I received an e-mail recently from someone who was theorising that in the moment before a sudden catastrophic death, there would have to be the seeing of liberation. We're always looking for cause and effect, for something that 'I' can do. Here the suggestion seems to be that we might throw ourself off a tall building, but I don't recommend it.

In any case, being asleep and being awake are the same thing, but this can't be seen while we are asleep. Another way of putting this is that it cannot be seen that there is no such thing as liberation until there is liberation. Of course, this is an awful paradox for the mind.

We think that something is going to be added on to us in liberation.

Yes, that's a very good way of putting it. We think that after liberation, I will still be me but now with new added super-ingredient 'Enlightenment!'

In liberation, nothing is changed yet everything is transformed. Everything stays the same but there is the recognition that there is no one seeing it.

I get concerned by the suggestion that this manifestation has no existence outside of us, that we are producing it. It seems quite an effort.

Don't worry that it will all dissolve if you relax. You're not doing it. This is only a metaphor but we could say that Oneness is doing it through you, that you are the projector through which Oneness shows the film.

Of course if you take enough drugs, it may all dissolve anyway. *(Laughter)*

2

The Box With The Key
Locked Inside

It's important to understand that this communication is completely impersonal. The seeing of liberation has nothing to do with the person. If there's anybody here who feels that this is about the possibility of personal liberation or enlightenment, then as long as you've paid, it's probably best that you leave right now.

It's very difficult for the mind to get hold of this point about impersonality. What is being communicated this afternoon is about something which is 'seen' but it's not seen by any individual. So there's no suggestion here that you or I can become liberated, enlightened or self-realised. Where there is a concept or a feeling that this is personal, the individual who's communicating this will usually be suggesting that they can do something about it for you, that they can somehow elevate you to a state that they have attained. Perhaps they can do this by divine transmission through you touching their holy feet, or drinking their bottled bathwater or worse, or they may offer to teach you spiritual techniques. We could practise spiritual techniques here but they wouldn't have anything to do with liberation.

As soon as this message gets caught up with the idea that it is somehow personal and you have a guru-devotee relationship developing, you get a collusion set up. You have someone who feels that they would like to become enlightened going to a teacher who offers them that. The teacher says "Yes, I have achieved enlightenment and I can give that to you. Come and sit at my feet, drink my bathwater, do my meditation techniques." You get a collusion between the devotee who wants to find an enlightened master and the teacher who wishes to present themselves as an enlightened master. They get together and pump each other up and that is when things tend to become very tricky. If we think that we can become enlightened, we may look for someone who is already enlightened who can somehow transfer their energy to us, whether through shaktipat or through some other means.

So this is a totally impersonal seeing. Although liberation may be seen, it is not seen by a person. Although separation can be seen through, it is not seen through by a person. A character may be sitting in this chair reporting on this but that's as close as we can get in language.

There is always impersonality but it is covered over by the sense of being an individual. Liberation is seen not when impersonality is gained but when the individual is lost.

This message is beyond mind or concepts or understanding. All we can do here is attempt to describe something and it will always be a failed attempt. We can share ideas about non-duality and somebody might go out of here having a very good understanding of it but that will have nothing to do with the seeing of non-duality. And there might be somebody down the road sitting in Hyde Park sunbathing this afternoon, who may have no ideas whatsoever about non-duality and yet suddenly there may simply be being. There may simply be sitting in Hyde Park but no one who is sitting.

Being is all that we are talking about today, simply being.

All I can offer this afternoon is to try to point towards liberation. We can never get there in words, we can't even get close, but we can point towards the simple reality of what is, the simple reality of being.

16

Let's acknowledge that all we can do here is tell a story, just as we're always telling stories about different aspects of being. Everything that we tell ourselves about the world and the purpose that we have in the world is a story. We tend to feel powerfully that we do have a purpose for being here. "Well, there must be something more than simply this! There just has to be! All of this palaver! All of these memories! All of this constant unreeling of thoughts! It must all be about something!" Our existence seems to have meaning and yet it is a story.

And this is also a story that we're telling this afternoon about non-duality. But although no story can touch reality, this is the one that points more directly to reality than any of the others. This one has the fewest decorative touches. The others start with being as it is, but on top of that they erect edifices. Some of these edifices can become incredibly complex. In the dream of time, they can be built up over thousands of years – Buddhism, Christianity, Advaita itself. And the more complex these edifices become, the less directly they point at the simplicity of being that is sitting here.

Think of some of the complex stories that you've come across like Tibetan Buddhism or Advaita-Vedanta and imagine what the opposite of those might be. It could be simply sitting here and noticing that there is being here, that there is life here. That's all we're talking about, simple being with all the narratives stripped away. That's what happens when liberation is impersonally seen. But liberation embraces everything, including those narratives themselves so I'm not suggesting that the stories of Buddhism and Christianity and Advaita-Vedanta are not also liberation.

It's possible as you sit here that for a while thought might drop away or awareness of some feeling in the body might no longer detain you. For a while there may just be the aware-ness of what is. That's all we're talking about. Or as you sit here it's possible that this doesn't happen, that a great deal of thinking may be going on or concepts may be swirling around or feelings may be arising. Perhaps there is anxiety about whether you remembered to turn the gas off, or anger about a parking warden you have had a row with. That's also what this is about. That's also being. That's liberation feeling anxious about turning off the gas or angry about the traffic warden. Or being may be thinking about Advaita-Vedanta. That's also what we're talking about. There might be an emptiness which just allows being to be, or a fullness with many thoughts and feelings and beliefs about the past and the future. It's all liberation.

But all the thoughts and feelings and concepts may go along with the sense of being a separate person. And although the sense of separation is also liberation, it's not felt to be the case. As long as the person feels separate, it will be felt that there is a problem. It will be felt that we are missing something, that there is something which we need to gain to make our life work so that we can feel satisfied. And if that's what's happening, there's no suggestion here that there's anyone who can do anything about it.

So there's only liberation, but within liberation there might arise a very powerful thought that "This isn't liberation! This is separation! There is a person here and I feel uncomfortable and dissatisfied. I feel that I've lost something and I want to find it again." The person wants to do something to end their dissatisfaction, their vulnerability and their separation. That can feel very uncomfortable and that may be what's happening right now.

If you want techniques, there are plenty of people out there offering techniques. You don't need yet another person here offering techniques. None of the hundreds of techniques have anything to do with liberation although many of them are very good at making the person feel more comfortable.

If there were a technique which could bring about liberation, I would put it in one word. I would say "Relax." That would be the supreme technique, the Maha-Technique, the mantra that would bear all souls to cosmic consciousness. "Relax." But there's no point in saying that because relaxation either happens or it doesn't. Maybe while being here this afternoon, relaxation will take place. Perhaps the mind, beating its head hopelessly against the wall of incomprehension which this communication is offering, will give up. But there's no guarantee of this at all. Instead, intense frustration might take place. I don't recommend intense frustration but it might happen. I recommend relaxation instead, but what can you do?

(Laughing) Maybe we'll try putting something in the tea.

There is no technique but if there were, it would be "Relax." We're doomed to failure, it's all hopeless, we are helpless, there is no meaning, there is no possibility of purpose, there is only despair, so we might as well relax and enjoy it. If only we could do that. If there were a technique, that would be it.

There are so many different things that are sometimes said about liberation, about how the past is seen through, how the future falls away, how regret and guilt tend to die away, how all the stories are seen through. But in a sense we can forget about all of that and we can especially forget about all the teachings. We can forget about everything except "Relax." In the seeing of liberation relaxation may take place.

It may be obvious that some of the stories that we entertain are not very conducive to relaxation if we take them seriously. If, for example, we take seriously the idea that we are going to burn in eternal hell-fire if we get our religion wrong and then that story drops away, perhaps you can see why there could be some relaxation. That could very well arise out of our no longer fearing eternal damnation. The expectation of hell-fire can be very stressful, particularly because in that kind of story everyone risks going to hell. All the Christians risk going to Muslim hell, all the Muslims risk going to Christian hell and all the Heathens and Nonbelievers risk spending six months of the year in each in a kind of infernal time-share.

I have a friend who has connections with a Baptist church. He meditates and his friends in the church are horrified. They think that he's emptying his mind and as far as they're concerned an empty mind is a space for evil spirits to come in. Satan is waiting to leap into the empty space created in his mind by meditation. If we have a paranoid belief like that and suddenly it falls away so that it is possible to see that it is just a story, that is quite likely to bring about some relaxation. If we have been walking around for forty years watching out for Satan over our shoulder and then we see through that story, it's likely that there'll be a mighty sigh of relief.

So if I could wish anything for you it would be to relax. But there isn't anything that can be done.

I have a short quote here. Back in the story of time in which there are famous American authors, Kurt Vonnegut died last week. You might not think this has any relevance but I do, although I'm sure Kurt Vonnegut was not interested in non-duality. This is what he says: "I tell you, we are here on Earth to fart around and don't let anybody tell you different." I don't feel like offering any further explanation of that. I feel it is self-evidently relevant. *(Laughter)* I cannot claim that the whole message of non-duality is contained in this quote but much of it is. When all the stories are seen through and this is seen for what it is and it's seen to be sufficient, then the farting around can not only begin, it can really be enjoyed.

Can you speak about how the body is seen through? It seems so strong, this feeling that I'm a person who has a body.

As long as 'we' are alive there is a body-mind. The mind is seen through very easily in liberation because what is seen is that the mind is not an entity, it is simply the process of thought. A thought arises and falls away and another thought arises. Usually, thoughts arise so rapidly and with so much energy that the impression is created that there is an entity, or a person, thinking them. The sense of 'I' is associated with these thoughts and with the impression that there is a mind. But in liberation , when much of the energy involved with thinking may dissipate, it may be easily seen that thoughts just arise from nothing.

But the body is still the body. Perhaps I hear in your question some sense that the body is a problem. But when this is seen, it is not a problem, it's just the body. In the world of phenomena there is still a physical separation. There is still an awareness that this arm is physically different to that table.

It's not a barrier to true unity?

Absolutely not, although I'm not sure what 'true' unity would mean. I'm suspicious of the word 'true'. But the body is definitely not a barrier. I don't know if it's helpful but I use the terms 'contraction' and 'localisation'. When there's a sense of separation, a sense of a person who isn't comfortable with simply being, this produces a sense of contraction. There's a sense of separation and vulnerability. We can be threatened and we have to protect ourself and negotiate with other separate individuals out there in the world. We've got to make sure that others don't trick us out of our money or steal our car. This sense of contraction can feel very uncomfortable. What happens when liberation is seen is that this sense of contraction can simply dissipate, rather in the same way that the energy of thought can dissipate.

You have to understand this is just metaphor, just the closest I can get in language to something impossible to describe. Try to imagine a translucent energy of awareness which is everywhere, and imagine that being coagulated down into a very precise personal awareness in a particular space. So now it seems that we are here in this particular space and these are *our* thoughts being generated by *our* mind. In a sense this is what the contracted feeling of being an individual is like. But it's not likely to be perceived in this way because the person has always lived with that feeling since the first moment they became self-conscious, so it's probably never been noticed. It's like not noticing the wallpaper that we've always lived with. Nevertheless we may feel uncomfortable in ourself, self-conscious, or even tormented.

When liberation is seen, this sense of tightness and contraction can dissipate. It can simply disappear in a moment. But what's left is still a sense of localisation unless liberation coincides with physical death. The body-mind organism still exists, probably complete with its character, its personality traits and its preferences. This all remains. It is Oneness appearing as a body-mind.

The feeling of contraction isn't something that anybody can do anything about. I want to say "Just forget about it. It doesn't matter." But I know it's useless to say this because there's no one who can forget about it. In other words, if it's going to be felt as a problem, it will be felt like that until it isn't. If there's a feeling of discomfort in the body, it will be there until it's gone.

I can try to stay relaxed and not think about the mind and enjoy being, enjoy what appears in the moment. But it's a kind of pretence for me to be beyond the mind. It feels like an effort.

As long as there's the sense of a person, then the person can only pretend to go beyond the mind. That's why I say that if there were a method it would be to relax. A person may make an effort to relax but 'making an effort to relax' is self-evidently absurd. Or there might be the thought that we have no thoughts, or the concept that we are simply being. That's just what it's like to be a person. When the person drops away, there is just thinking, just being and just seeing.

It's not true that I didn't come here to get anything. I'm jealous because you see liberation.

No, I don't see liberation.

O.K. Liberation is seen.

But not by me.

O.K. Not by you.

I'm sure I could tell you enough salient characteristics of my life so you'll no longer feel jealous. *(Laughter)* What's your name?

Maria.

You might think "Thank God I'm Maria and not Richard." The point is that this has nothing to do with Richard. There's nothing to feel jealous of because there's no one to feel jealous of. Richard isn't liberated. Richard doesn't even see liberation. Liberation is simply seen. Richard's life might be very dull compared to Maria's. We could swap notes in the tea break.

I don't care whether your life is dull. It's the seeing of Oneness that I want. It appears that you as a body-mind can speak about liberation with a strong sense of knowing what it is and what it isn't. I can't.

You can probably speak about something else that I can't speak about. Are you Italian?

Yes.

Then you can probably speak Italian quite a lot better than I can. I'm not being frivolous. This is so paradoxical. I want to say "I can talk liberation, you can talk Italian. So what?" But I recognise that when there is a person feeling separate and thinking that there is something to attain that can end that feeling, these are the kind of thoughts that arise. There's nothing that I can suggest that you do about that because there is no Maria who can do anything.

****

I think that when we get to a certain age there's a sense of wanting to come home. There's no dispute here about what you're saying. It's exactly right. But I still feel an enormous frustration. I've been engaged with a spiritual path for forty years and when people like you sit out at the front and say there's nothing we can do, it's quite painful. Because we want to come home. That's basically why we're sitting here. And coming home is presumably hindered by the sense of separation.

No it isn't.

But it's the ultimate paradox that we're trying to open the box with the key locked inside it. And we can't do it. Which suggests that there is almost a certain cruelty about this. There's a randomness about it. There may be some guy who is in his twenties and who has never been interested in philosophy or spirituality at all, and suddenly he's enlightened.

No he isn't.

O.K. Suddenly there is enlightenment. But I, who have been engaged in trying to wake up for forty years and have a very good intellectual understanding of the teachings, still am not able to get it. And inevitably this makes me angry because of the randomness of the situation. In any other situation, if we were studying music for example, we would be a master after forty years.

But this has nothing to do with us. It has nothing to do with the mind. It has nothing to do with understanding. It's not given to anybody as a reward. In fact, it's not given to anybody. No young guy in his twenties ever became enlightened. That's not what happens, but it seems to be what happens to the mind, to the person. The person may think "The most powerful tool I have for understanding the world is my mind. It's enabled me to comprehend all kinds of wonderful things: French, Spirituality, Quantum Mechanics." But there seems to be this thing called liberation which the mind can't get any purchase on whatsoever. Of course that can be experienced as frustrating and annoying. It can make us angry and seem totally unfair. Everything in our life tells us that we can get somewhere with work and effort, that we can get to some desired goal, whether we're training to be a taxi driver or a concert pianist. But there is apparently this ultimate desired goal called liberation and the mind can get nowhere with it.

Of course it can feel unfair, but it isn't unfair because there is no one who will ever become liberated. And even the seeing of liberation confers no benefit and brings no reward to a person.

I have just given an interview in which I assert that you're better off with a cup of tea than with liberation. *You* are better off with a cup of tea because *you* can drink a cup of tea but *you* can't do anything with liberation.

It really has no reward?

Not for *you*. It has no reward for a person.

But the reward is that you've come home. Or there is a coming home.

Apparently.

Is that not what you're saying?

Apparently there is a coming home but actually there never was a leaving home in the first place. The seeing of liberation is the giving up of all seeking because apparently there is a coming home so there's no longer anything to seek. But in fact it's seen that there never had been anything to seek.

There is no coming home because we never left it.

But for a person, I relate to what you're saying. I not only relate to it, I can remember in the story of Richard having many of these same thoughts and feelings myself.

You could say "Well, if there's nothing I can do I might as well get drunk."

But there's no one who can choose that. There may be the character of an alcoholic or of a spiritual seeker there. That has nothing to do with 'you'. There's nothing personal about it. Actually, there's nothing personal about any of our character traits. I've already said that liberation is impersonal. So is everything else. If there's a tendency to go out and get drunk every night, that is as impersonal as liberation. Coming here is also impersonal. No one made any choice to come here today because there is no one. Impersonality arises here as the appearance of a group of people talking about non-duality.

The first time I read about non-duality a few months ago, I was really scared. It was really a shock. I thought "I don't exist. My husband doesn't exist. What's going on?" I was sad. But now I've come to a more peaceful relationship with Advaita. So there's a desire for liberation but up to what point? Because I like the story. There is something that doesn't want to leave the story, that is attached to it. The story can be beautiful. Maybe Oneness really likes the story.

It must do. Why else would all this be happening? But what you're reporting is very common. Often people discover this, get a little close to it and then run away from it. This is a fire that burns through everything. It cuts through everything. We may come to this with our story, perhaps of an evolutionary spiritual path, for example. We get close to this, we recognise on some level what it is saying and so we don't come back. We recognise that we would have to give up the wonderful story that we are going to become an enlightened being in about ten lifetimes and then we will be a bodhisattva and we'll teach others to become enlightened beings. This can just be too attractive to give up. So instead we run away from the threat that this presents.

The fear of the story dropping away is very common. But although I don't want to suggest that there is any reward or any necessary implications in seeing liberation, nevertheless when liberation is seen, the story might really be enjoyed for the first time. Because now it can be enjoyed simply as a story, now there's no longer any personal investment in it because there's no person to be invested in it.

Whether it is Tibetan Buddhism or the thirty-seven different levels of Quantum Enlightenment, it is possible that if liberation is seen, that story will just fall away and there'll be no interest in it anymore. But it's also possible that the interest may still be there. Perhaps we like the other people involved, we love the guru, we adore going to Nevada where his ashram is and for the first time we can really enjoy all of it simply as it is, because there's no longer any craving to get something from it.

In Buddhism they talk about craving being an impediment to peace of mind. Well, they're damned right. Craving is an impediment. However we can't do anything to give craving up because we do not exist. Nevertheless craving can drop away. If craving for the state of the bodhisattva or for personal enlightenment drops away because liberation is seen, the story without craving may really be enjoyed.

There's no necessity for the stories to disappear. Sometimes they do. Sometimes they don't. Here a lot of stories have disappeared, so I sit around stroking the cats and I walk around the park and drink coffee on the verandah of the café. But perhaps mine is a particularly lazy body-mind.

If worry about the possible absence of stories arises, it arises. Nothing can be done. But I can sit here and say "Don't worry about that because Surprise! Surprise! The story might really feel delicious once it's seen through." Can you imagine getting in amongst the Baptists who are saying "Don't empty your mind or Satan will leap in" and playing along with that while seeing through it? It might be great fun. Or you might just think "I can't be bothered with that. I'll sit at home and stroke the cats instead of going to church."

When you talk you use terms like 'I', 'me' and 'you'.

It's just the nature of language. If we to try to avoid these terms we end up torturing language. It sounds awful. We can end up with people trying to talk as if they're not people.

I have lucid dreams. I know I'm dreaming and I sometimes wonder whether life is like a lucid dream.

Lucid dreaming is a good metaphor because it involves a waking up to the realisation that it is a dream. First there is a dream going on, which appears to be reality. Then within that dream there is a kind of waking up. The person having the dream remains asleep, but there is now an awareness that it is a dream. That is a good metaphor for liberation. The seeing of liberation is like being asleep in a night-time dream and suddenly becoming aware that it is a dream. Not that I am dreaming, but that it is a dream. Liberation is the seeing that this is all a dream including the person who appears to be dreaming. I am a dreamed character and so I do not wake up. There is simply an awakening to lucidity.

Where there is a person with a sense of separation, there appears to be an 'I' who is totally caught up in the dream. But in

27

liberation it is seen that it is all a dream, including the person who is apparently having the dream.

But it's impossible for us to see that this is a dream and we are a dreamed character?

Yes, as long as there's the sense of a person there. As long as there's the sense of a separate person, it can't be seen that this is a dreamed character. There can be an understanding of concepts about it, there can even be an agreement with it, but there can't be the seeing of it.

It's very easy to see through your night-time dreams when you wake up in the morning. You might have been racing to catch a train in your dream but the moment you wake up that is seen through. Then it's seen that the 'you' in the dream who felt so real was just an appearance. This day-time dream is like racing for the train in the night-time dream for as long as there is the sense of a person. But in awakening it is seen through.

Sometimes during the day-time you suddenly wake up just as you might in the night. Not permanently but for a little while.

During the day we may be taking something very seriously and then suddenly we might see through it. We may be terribly angry and then we might catch sight of the cat walking across the room and the anger can just be gone. At a moment like that, we can sometimes see through the story.

Phenomena simply arise out of Oneness and fall away. Anger arises and falls away. A cat walking across the room arises and falls away. Fear about a doctor's appointment arises and falls away. A cup of tea arises and falls away. We think we have something to do with all this. But we don't have anything to do with it because we're not here.

This display of phenomena is very convincing. It is very good at creating the appearance of a person who is involved in it and active in it and who makes choices about it. It's very good at creating the sensation that there's a person at the centre of all of this.

****

When this is seen it may create a sense of detachment.

It may do.

That was my fear, that I might feel detached from my friends, my family, my loved ones. When the story is seen for what it is, I fear I will not love anyone anymore because I will not exist and that is painful.

The person may think "My God, I could lose everything!" You will lose everything because you'll lose you. But that may not be as gloomy as it sounds. You were asking earlier about relationship. I could say "There is no relationship" and that could sound scary. But I might add "But there's relating." In the same way, I said there's no mind but there's thinking. So there's no relationship in the sense of a concept or an entity, but there's a process of relating. And it's possible that when relationship is seen through, then relating might be more intimate. At least be open to the possibility that this may be the case. Relating without relationship may be deeper and more intimate because there's no longer a concept or an entity coming between you.

If liberation is seen here this afternoon by you and your husband, if that happens for both of you, firstly I want you to give me all of your money. *(Laughter)* But apart from that, if liberation is suddenly seen, there will still be two body-minds, two characters, two personalities. There's the possibility that those two body-minds may be more intimate because there's no longer the concept of relationship there. Concepts don't tend to bring us into intimate closeness. So what might disappear, paradoxically, could be something that actually keeps these two body-minds apart. If there's a sense of separation in each of you, there will be a sense of separation between you. So you could hold it as a possibility that in the disappearance of the self, relating could become stronger. And you don't need to worry about love because everything's love anyway. There is only love. It will take care of itself. I know that

29

when you look at some aspects of the drama that are going on in the world, this seems unlikely and you might say "How could that possibly be love?" But it is.

It seems so unfair that somebody can get the jackpot of enlightenment just by lying in the park and doing nothing.

Let's say that for forty years we've been running around the hamster wheel of a spiritual path or heaving ourself painfully up the rock-face of enlightenment mantra by mantra with scraped knees and occasional broken bones. And someone lying in the sun in Hyde Park who's never done any of that gets it. That seems very unfair. But in the seeing of liberation, it's realised that there never were those forty years of running round the hamster wheel of personal enlightenment so it isn't unfair. Those forty years are just a thought. It's easy to lose sight of this, but when liberation is seen, of course there's no unfairness because there was nobody who ever did any of that. It's just a passing thought arising in this.

When I leave these meetings, I never know what's been said. But it feels like something's happened energetically.

No matter what's going on, there's always something happening energetically.

Can techniques like 'Being In The Now' be helpful in bringing about liberation?

It's very common for people to feel that they can help others to awaken by teaching them techniques. This is a confusion that arises when someone feels that liberation is personal to them and they can make it personal for you. A lot of spiritual communication is of this nature. At its heart lies the idea that "I have got to the end of the path, or at least further along the path than you have, and I can teach you how to get there as well."

There's nothing wrong with saying this but it happens to be totally misleading.

And remember that for the seeker, it can be very seductive to be told that there is something you can teach me which will bring liberation closer to me.

You can't really judge a technique from the outside. If Oneness suddenly starts breathing me ...

Oneness is already breathing you. Right now. And if you decide to do a breathing technique, that's Oneness doing a breathing technique. There's nothing wrong with that. But it has nothing to do with liberation, except that it's also liberation. You are a character dreamed by Oneness, breathed by Oneness, spoken by Oneness. You are Oneness drinking cups of tea.

Doing techniques is fine. I could teach you some techniques, for an enormous amount of money. But they won't get you closer to seeing liberation. I could sell you a mantra, a new mantra or a used mantra. I could sell you a second-hand mantra with less than one hundred thousand repetitions on the clock. And it would be good. It would work. But it would have nothing to do with liberation. Except that meditating on one of Richard's second-hand mantras is also liberation. It's liberation being somewhat confused and deluded. But most of the time liberation is somewhat confused and deluded. That's what keeps much of the game going. It's a great game of confusion and delusion and sometimes it's fun. That's why many people feel that they don't really want to give it up. Among all the angst and the pain and the searching, it's actually quite fun as well.

There's only Oneness so every phenomenon that arises is Oneness. Delusion is Oneness. Confusion is Oneness. Meditating is Oneness. Buying one of Richard's second-hand mantras is Oneness.

What happened in your story? How did it come about that Oneness decided to reveal itself to you?

There was a momentary event in which the complete emptiness of the self was seen. The Buddhists talk about seeing the emptiness of all phenomena. It's the seeing that I am nothing, that there is no 'I'. That first seeing had a kind of coldness and detachment about it because it was simply empty. It had a rather masculine energy to it. 'Empty phenomena rolling by' doesn't sound very warm and loving, does it?

Nevertheless at the time it was felt that this seeing was complete. But then the person came back and was pretty unhappy and was still searching, hoping to see that emptiness again for longer and longer, hoping it would become permanent. In other words, there was a misunderstanding of that awakening event. Later on there was another event when the person disappeared again and everything that had remained as a puzzle dropped away. In this second event, everything that was empty was also seen to be full. That sounds paradoxical but it can't be helped. Emptiness is full of love even if sometimes it doesn't look like that to a person.

In these events all sense of personal identity disappeared. It was seen that there is only awareness. That wall is just as much awareness as this person is. Later, the sense of localisation came back so it was felt once again that there was a body-mind, but the sense of separation and contraction had gone.

Isn't it just another experience?

An experience is something that happens to a person. This is not an experience because it doesn't happen to a person. It can't be an experience because there's nobody there to be having an experience. That's why I call it an event. 'Event' isn't an accurate word either because 'event' implies that there's something happening, but actually there's nothing happening.

Is it a peak experience?

No, it's not a peak experience. A peak experience happens to a person. It might be a person who's attained a very refined, almost translucent state for a while but it's still a person.

Is it a spiritual experience?

This has got nothing to do with spiritual experiences. There's nothing more spiritual about awakening and liberation than about anything else. It might sound spiritual, however, because of the words we have to use, such as saying that everything is love.

I wouldn't associate this with spirituality, but if you want to, that's fine.

I would say that an experience is something that's transient.

Yes, it's transient and it happens to a person. Liberation doesn't happen to a person. And it's outside time so any idea of it being either transient or permanent is irrelevant. This is also outside time. There might be a memory that we were drinking cups of tea in the sun earlier, but this is all there is and that memory simply arises in this. If reality has any meaning, this is the only meaning it has. This is it. This is the only reality. This is all that reality consists of, outside time.

What about this message itself? This seems to be taking place in time.

This message takes place within an apparent story within the dream which includes the dream of time. But the message is beyond time. That's why I'm saying that those events that this voice is apparently recalling are neither permanent nor transient. Both permanency and transience have to do with time. But nothing is either permanent or transient because there is no time.

What creates the impression of time is thought. Thought appears to exist in time because it appears to take time to have a thought, just as it appears to take time for me to say this sentence.

But it's possible for us to stop our thoughts. There are techniques for doing that.

The character who feels themself to be a person can learn techniques to slow down thoughts or stop them for a while. They tend to be mentally constipating so I don't recommend them. Within the dream in which there appears to be cause and effect, doing an effective meditation technique may tend to produce fewer thoughts. But that doesn't have anything to do with liberation.

One common thing that happens with spiritual paths is that there is a confusion between cause and effect. It is sometimes noticed when liberation is seen that the energy of thought may dissipate. There may be fewer thoughts, quieter thoughts, less energised thoughts. It may also be noticed when liberation is seen that it's possible for a certain detachment to arise. After all, if I'm not taking the story seriously anymore, that might produce some detachment. These are possible consequences of liberation, they don't necessarily occur.

Commonly in spiritual schools this is all turned on its head and the consequences are perceived as causes rather than effects. If I am looking for somebody who can teach me how to become personally enlightened, I may come across a guru who seems to have some detachment and who seems to have a quiet mind. I might think "I want that. He can teach me how to be like that. He can teach me techniques which will make me detached and give me a quiet mind. Then I'll be closer to liberation." So developing detachment and a quiet mind become seen as techniques which can produce liberation. That is exactly the wrong way round. Seeing liberation may produce a quieter mind and more detachment.

In Buddhism there is often an emphasis on producing a quiet mind. Some people suggest that this is the result of a mistranslation or a misunderstanding. The original meaning may have been not that a quiet mind is a path to liberation but that liberation may produce a quieter mind.

Detachment is extremely appealing to some people, particularly to many men. It's possible that if I have a certain spiritual or ascetic mind-set, I may look for a guru who appears to be detached, who's celibate, who doesn't eat bloody steaks, who doesn't go ten-pin bowling and who doesn't drink whisky. This is a very attractive idea. Detachment is sometimes seen as a necessity in a spiritually evolved being.

If for five years I follow a guru who appears to be detached and then I discover that he's having sex with some of his devotees, he's drinking whisky like it is milk and he's eating raw steaks three times a day, then I'm likely to be quite disappointed. But it's almost inevitable that if we deny something in ourselves, it will come out in a negative way. We'll either project it onto other people or it will manifest itself in an addictive or otherwise unhealthy way. If there's a guru who has this wonderful detachment, but he's also surrounded by gorgeous blonde devotees, it's quite likely that he'll be finding his way to the women's dormitory through a secret tunnel every night.

Because he's human?

Of course.

It's up to us how much power we give to the guru.

Yes. But who could resist the offer of the special darshan, the darshan that opens and purifies the lower chakras? *(Laughter)*

****

You mentioned the confusion of cause and effect. Is liberation an uncaused event?

Everything is uncaused. Everything spontaneously arises and falls away. This mug of tea is uncaused. It's a spontaneous mug of tea. But the mind looks for causation. When I talk about the confusion of cause and effect, I mean that this occurs within the story, within the dream of a person looking for a spiritual path. That's where cause and effect get confused. One of the easiest ways to see that there really is no cause is to notice how a thought arises and falls away. And then how another thought comes and falls away. Thoughts arise without cause or significance, but if there's a person there, that person may give those thoughts great significance.

That sounds like a technique to me.

(Laughing) Oh no! Shoot me now! What sounds like a technique?

Notice thoughts.

No, It's not a technique. That's just how you heard it. It won't do you or anybody else any good. It's just a way of trying to explain that everything is uncaused. After all, this chair seems very solid so we may think "How can that be uncaused? Somebody made that chair." I'm just suggesting that it may be easier to notice that thoughts are uncaused. It's possible that, as you sit here, there may be a moment of no mental activity. Then it may be noticed that, totally uncaused, the next thought comes. That's not a technique. It won't get you anywhere.

No one's here to notice it?

No one's here to notice it and no one can get anywhere by noticing it.

Certain people think God caused it.

Some people do, yes. That's a very attractive story. It makes sense to millions of people.

But in a way, what does seeing that this is uncaused change? There is only Oneness and Oneness contains crap gurus, uncaused chairs and lots of stories. I feel like judging lots of things because I know they're crap, but on the other hand I don't want to judge them because they're all part of Oneness.

There's nothing wrong with judging. You say "I don't want to

36

judge" and that's fine. But judging is just part of Oneness. I'm very judgemental.

That's what I wanted to hear.

Are you happy now? *(Laughter)*

Yes, I feel better now. You've got some faults.

If we're going to start listing my faults we'll be here for hours. This particular personality can be highly judgemental, but I wouldn't say that being judgemental is a fault. But remember that this communication has nothing to do with this character except for its flavour.

I need to make some compromise with the story. I can't live my daily life without compromising with the story.

Your daily life is already simply being lived. You have never lived your daily life.

I'm a passive recipient of life? Life is living through me?

Of course. It may seem that you are doing something, but life is just living through you.

But I have to compromise in the story because I can't live life think- ing everything is uncaused.

Why not? Do you feel your life would stop if you didn't compro- mise with that? It wouldn't. But sometimes people think that it would.

No, it's nothing like that with me. But why do you call it a story?

Words are difficult, but the word 'story' is an attempt to acknowl- edge that there does seem to be something going on. Phenomena do seem to arise. Saying that it's a story, or a dream, or an appearance, is a way of trying to acknowledge that it's both real and not real. Just as nothing is either permanent or transient, we could also say that everything is both real and unreal. It's real in the sense that it does apparently arise. There's no doubt about that. But it's unreal in the sense that it's seen in liberation that nothing has ever happened, nothing will ever happen and nothing is happening right now. There is also no 'right now' in which anything can happen. That's why I call it a story, a dream, maya, a game, a play, an appearance. These are all words that try to express the perception that there appears to be something and yet there is only nothing.

****

The thought of death is very disturbing, though not so much when it's the death of somebody I don't know. Death seems to put me very much in touch with what you're talking about. I can't explain that intellectually but it's a very clear sensation.

Our own death absolutely confronts us with the reality that this is a story. Other people's deaths can also confront us with that. It is precisely the existence of death in the dream that makes so many of us make up these wild, wild stories about the things that must be achieved and the heavens that must be aimed for. For a person, death is quite a challenge, so to avoid contemplating its own annihilation, the mind makes up the most wonderful and bizarre stories about an entity that continues after death in some way.

Nothing continues after death but that's ok because nothing is continuing right now.

When people have suffered a bereavement and they go to psychics, they often feel relief. They feel that their dead loved ones are around them somewhere. They accept it, they feel they've had evidence and that's good enough for them. I quite envy them in a way. So sometimes when you say there's nothing afterwards ...

There's nothing before either. This is nothing.

If there's nothing before ...

And there's no before and no after because there's no time.

Then that psychic stuff is actually no less real than this.

Yes. It's all phenomena arising in this.

So Uncle Fred and Aunt Lizzie are telling us something from the other side?

No.

So what's real?

Whatever phenomena are arising. The phenomenon that arises may be the voice of a psychic reporting on something that Aunt Lizzie is saying from beyond the grave. But that's got nothing to do with Aunt Lizzie being beyond the grave. It's just the phenomenon that is arising, just as here cups of tea and talking about non-duality are arising.

But I may feel that I know that it's real, that it really is Aunt Lizzie.

Then what's arising is your acceptance that this story has some kind of reality to it. This chair has no reality to it except in the dream but it seems solid enough. Many people are desperate for a story that says there is a reality here that will continue beyond death. It doesn't matter whether the story is Christianity, Islam or Clairvoyance, there will be a desperation to find a story that provides that meaning. Other people might really envy someone who has accepted one of those stories. It can provide a complete answer to everything. Until it doesn't. Then you're in trouble. If there's a person there and the story that has provided meaning falls away, then often the person is confronted with all the existential issues. If meaning drops away but there's still a person there, then you're likely to be left in the desert or in the dark night of the soul.

But as long as the meaningful story can be sustained, it's wonderful. You could go on visiting clairvoyants and talking to Aunt Lizzie for ever.

I understand that all that stuff is comforting but what about karma? I used to find it so beguiling because there's justice involved. When you die, your body goes back to earth and your mind goes to universal mind. But your heart continues until it takes up another body. That is lawful and reasonable and within the story it makes a lot of sense. Otherwise how is it decided that we're going to sit here in the West and be well-fed and some poor soul in Africa is going to be starving? What's wrong with it?

Everything you've said about karma makes sense. It's deeply satisfying compared to a lot of the other stories because it seems to fulfil our desire for justice and everything eventually sorts itself out. There's nothing wrong with it. But it's a story made up by the mind. What we're talking about here is beyond the mind.

What about suffering? Somebody's raped. Or there's extreme poverty.

Ultimately there are only a very few things that can be said about suffering. All the many questions about suffering come down essentially to three. These are "How can I relieve my own suffering?", "How can the suffering of other people be relieved?" and "What is the meaning of suffering?"

"How can I relieve my own suffering?" There are lots of techniques that can help to relieve your own suffering. Of course, there's no one who can do anything about it but doing one of these techniques might be what happens.

"How can the suffering of other people be relieved?" If you are concerned about the suffering of others, it's obvious that there are lots of things that can be done about that. You can collect for charity, drive trucks to Africa, feed the poor, work politically for a fairer world.

"What is the meaning of suffering?" If you want a story about the meaning of suffering, then choose a religion. There are lots of them out there. Choose the one that most appeals to you, maybe one that involves karma. They're the most rational ones. However, all of them fall apart when it's seen that there's no one, no volition, no choice, no free will and nothing has ever happened. Then karma is seen through like all the other stories.

Did you know that the more rapidly you get your karmic come-backs, the more spiritually evolved you are supposed to be? I have a friend whose wife ran off many years ago. She is now living in Germany. He heard recently that she'd had quite a serious flood in her house and he could not help a feeling of glee arising in his heart. Ten minutes later he went upstairs and discovered that his own roof was leaking. That's instant karma. It's supposed to show that he's a very highly evolved spiritual being. If you have a low level of spiritual evolution it can take years, or even lifetimes, for your karma to come to fruition.

Can you see how these stories develop? They're so attractive. They always revolve around the idea that I am getting somewhere. "I get my karma instantly so I'm highly spiritually evolved." It's the madness of the mind. The mind never tires of inventing these wonderful but insane stories.

****

Tell us about Mathieu Ricard. You mentioned him in the tea-break.

Mathieu Ricard is a French Tibetan Buddhist monk. He's very close to the Dalai Lama. He's been a celibate monk for thirty years.

Somebody was talking about going on a Tai Chi weekend the other day and they suggested that it might involve celibacy. Someone else said "What! Celibacy, for a whole weekend!" *(Laughter)*

41

Mathieu Ricard has just written a book called 'Happiness'. There's now a place in America where they can test your happiness level by taking readings of your brain-wave patterns. He is almost off the scale. On the scale of least happy to most happy he is right up at the top. They describe him as the happiest man they've ever tested. Presumably he is so happy because he does Tibetan Buddhist practices.

I heard Mathieu Ricard being interviewed on the radio and he sounded like a lovely man. But I felt that in a way this could easily become another oppression. This suggestion, that we are not happy enough and we can become happier, gives us something else to seek. You might say "Surely everybody wants to be happy." Yes, every person does, but liberation has got nothing to do with happiness. Liberation is way beyond happiness. When I say that it's way beyond happiness, I don't mean it's bliss. I just mean it's way beyond happiness. Happiness is seen to be irrelevant.

I did feel a bit ignoble having this reaction. What could possibly be the harm in suggesting that we can become happier? But I thought "It's another oppression. It's something else to do. It's something else possibly to fail at and to feel inadequate about." If I suggest to you that there are practices that you can do to become happier and that you need to do these for your spiritual growth, what is the essential message I'm giving you? I'm telling you that this isn't it. This isn't enough and you're not good enough.

Then I had a vision of going on a Buddhist Happiness Retreat and sitting there consumed with envy at all the other students who were clearly better at being happy than I was. *(Laughter)* I'd probably be interviewed by the head monk at the end of the retreat and I'd be awash with guilt and inadequacy and a sense of failure because I hadn't managed to be happy enough. And now they have machines to test you, so I couldn't even lie about it!

Everybody would know! (Laughter)

Everybody would know! It would be like getting your exam results. The monks would post the brain-wave readings on a notice board so everyone could see them. They'd be saying "Oo, look at Richard! He's not very happy! And he calls himself a non-duality communicator!"

So even this very innocent suggestion that we can do techniques to become happier can feel like an oppression. It's another suggestion that this isn't it. It's something else we can do to get somewhere else, to get somewhere where we aren't now.

I was listening to a Quaker recently. He read out an improving passage from a Quaker book of readings. It was about how we must use every moment we are on the earth to become more aware and to become more loving to others and to develop and improve ourselves. It's so tiring! I would rather place my faith in farting around as Kurt Vonnegut said.

Fart around. If there were a technique, I'd say at five o'clock, which isn't all that far away, let's all go out and fart around. But don't feel failed if you don't fart around enough.

My mind just came up with this statement: "The less of a person I am, the more successful at this I am." That monk's selling happiness. I think "I come here and the less of a person I am, the more I'm getting this." But it's impossible for me to become less of a person.

We have a brain-wave meter at the door and we're going to measure you as you leave to see how much of the person has dropped away. *(Laughter)* We'll grade you and we'll stick the grades on the wall at the next meeting.

The mind is wonderful at picking up any idea and distorting it or turning it into something which becomes another task, which will prove to the mind "This isn't it. How could this be it? It's too ordinary!" Actually, it's not.

So can you still feel like a person when you're awakened?

You're not awakened. I mean no one is, I'm not picking on you. *(Laughter)* No one is awakened. But it depends what you mean by 'feel like a person'. Phenomena continue to arise and many of them may be connected to what it feels like to be a person, such as thoughts, feelings and physical sensations. But when liberation is seen, it is seen that these phenomena are not attached to a person. They simply arise.

Remember that some phenomena, including ones that are quite uncomfortable, could arise more strongly when there's no person there. Forget any idea that there is some sort of enlightened state in which uncomfortable feelings cannot arise. Dudjom Rinpoche said "Even in the greatest yogi, sorrow and joy still arise just as before." Any feeling can still arise, possibly more strongly, because a person, particularly if they're quite neurotic, can set up defences against experiencing feelings in the raw. For example, a person will often not allow themself to fully feel or to enjoy their anger. They'll often feel irritation or annoyance instead because that's safer. Or they might never allow themself to feel fear. They'll only allow themself to feel anxiety, because anxiety feels safer than fear. So it's possible that when the person's not there anymore, there might be anger and fear instead of irritation and anxiety. But it doesn't matter. It's o.k.

What about someone like Ramana Maharshi who you hear all these stories about, the gurus' guru? Or Nisargadatta? The story is that they're in bliss all the time. Are there different levels of enlightenment? Is there something special about Ramana Maharshi or Nisargadatta compared to, dare I say, you? (Laughter)

(Laughing) Please don't compare me unfavourably to Nisargadatta or Ramana Maharshi.

So what's going on there?

The mind constructs stories all the time to keep a goal out there so that the person can keep moving towards it. The story might be about shopping or losing weight or religion. But if it's a spiritual story it is often maintained by setting up an impossible ideal. Because it's an impossible ideal, we can never reach it and so we can keep moving along the spiritual path towards it forever.

We could regard this as simply the activity of psychological projection. We disown all our most positive qualities and make ourself into a miserable, inadequate, unenlightened spiritual seeker. Then we project all our positive qualities onto a guru. The more idealised we make the guru and the more unattainable his state seems, the longer we can maintain our search. We project all our idealised longings onto the guru until he lets us down, which he probably will. He'll probably be caught eventually with the whisky bottle or the attractive blondes. Then we will often transfer our projected longings onto a different guru. The ultimate joy with someone like Ramana Maharshi is he's dead. *(Laughter)* Seriously! We aren't going to catch him in the women's dormitory. So in a sense a dead guru is the best guru. He will never let us down just as Shakespeare will never write a bad play. So we can continue to project all of our yearnings onto him.

Pretending for the moment that there was a past in which Ramana Maharshi existed, I have no idea what state he was in. It might have been a state of extreme detachment. Who cares? It's irrelevant. This is it. This is enough. We don't need Ramana Maharshi.

We seem to need validation from another person.

As long as that need's there, it's there. When this is seen as sufficient, it's seen as sufficient. While there's a person there, if they have a certain very common psychological mind-set, they may well search for validation. If they're hoping for spiritual evolution, they might go to a guru who seems able to validate them, who can say "Yes, you've come a certain way along the path. But not as far as I've come!" A different person might decide to evolve by studying logical-positivism. Their validation might come from their philosophy professor. It makes no difference.

We're out of time, folks.

I will buy your book.

Thank you. Now I will be able to eat tonight! *(Laughter)*

3

First Plant One Apple Tree

We are here to talk about nothing less than the end of the sense that there is a person.

The sense that I am a separate person in a sometimes alien world gives rise to certain inescapable thoughts and feelings. Chief amongst these, apart from 'I exist', is the feeling that I am able to make autonomous choices, that I have a life which I am in charge of in some way, that I am the executive director of a project called 'my life'.

Many of us go through life oscillating between grandiosity and despair. Some of us settle on one of these positions. The degree of autonomy that we feel will depend on the position that we adopt as we try to negotiate our life. If our position is despair, we may adopt the role of a victim. This is a surprisingly popular role in which we see our choices as very limited. We will see circumstances, other people or our accursed fate as controlling us and imposing suffering on us. But even for someone in a victim role there will be some sense of choice, some sense of negotiating the blighted wasteland of our life through the exercise of our own free will.

In grandiosity, a magnificently arrogant role may be adopted. One way this emerges is in our many determined beliefs that we can ultimately understand (or already now understand) the mystery and miracle of this incredible manifestation. Some of the stories told about this require us to believe in a God whose intentions and preferences we know. We may believe that we know who God wants us to smite and who should be left unsmitten.

Or some of the stories might be scientific ones. We might believe that because we have understood something about the mechanics of memory and perception, we have explained consciousness. Or because we have developed a coherent theory about the Big Bang, we have explained the existence of everything.

A scientist with more humility and an appreciation of the mystery of life was quoted on the radio recently. He'd written a recipe for making apple pie. It began

'First, plant one apple tree.'

and it went on

'In order to do this, you will need to create a planet.'

This reminded me of the story of a group of scientists who went to God and said "We don't need you anymore. We've discovered how to make life from dirt, just like you did." God said "That's very interesting. Why don't you show me how you do it?" So one of the scientists bent down and started scooping some dirt up from the ground. God said "Oi! What do think you're doing!" The scientist said "I'm getting some dirt ready." God said "That's my dirt! You create your own!"

Without humility, we do not notice that in our explanations of how things are there is always an infinite regression back to that which cannot be explained.

Another scientist with humility, a psychologist, contributed a definition of consciousness to a dictionary of psychology. It was extremely short and it ended with the line "Nothing worth reading about this has ever been written." And a cognitive psychologist has written "Psychology is not ready to tackle the issue of consciousness." We might be tempted to add "And it never will be ready."

Whether we are arrogant or whether we are humble, whatever our belief system, there is almost always a belief in choice. In existentialism, for example, there is a great deal of emphasis on choice and it is held that even in the most restricted circumstances, the individual always has some ability to exercise free will. We may be tied to a stake, blindfolded, with ten rifle muzzles pointing at a target pinned to our chest, but it is felt that we still have a choice about how, for example, we orientate our thoughts and feelings towards this event. We can choose to face our imminent death bravely, to die defying our enemies, to regard our blood as being shed for a worthy cause. This is, of course, a very heroic story.

The idea that through choice we can make our life work is a very gripping one, even though the choices we apparently make are sometimes rather counterintuitive. We might be a little baffled about how we could ever have thought that drinking our tenth bottle of vodka this week would make our life work. Nevertheless there is this sense: "I am here. It's sometimes quite difficult being on this planet. I can make choices and these choices may have the effect of making this stuff called life easier to handle." Our choices might be about getting a better job, drinking more vodka, finding a partner, buying a dog, going to live in an ashram. There will be a sense that these choices can have an effect on this huge work of fiction known as 'My Life'.

But essentially it doesn't matter what the choice seems to be about because it is in any case unreal.

In liberation, it is seen that all of this story of choice, autonomy and individual action is an incredibly persuasive fiction. Because there is no separate individual, there is no choice. The thought that we exist as a separate entity and we make choices is just another phenomenon that arises.

Of course there are many other stories about liberation which can be very attractive. One of the most attractive is that liberation will confer on us a permanent state of bliss. It's a wonderful thought, though unfortunately it's contradicted by the evidence of our entire lifetime, which shows clearly that everything is impermanent. Impermanence is one of the most obvious characteristics of existence. Everything is quite clearly in a constant state of change, of flux.

Nevertheless, the idea of permanent bliss through the attainment of a state of personal enlightenment can be so alluring that we may remain deluded by it. We may ignore our fifty or sixty years of experience that tells us that everything constantly changes.

A thought or a feeling may last for a few seconds. A cup of tea might last slightly longer. The fact that nothing is permanent, including bliss, is always staring us in the face.

There are other stories told about personal enlightenment. We may believe that this state can confer extraordinary wisdom on us, or magical powers, great insight, or an attractive golden aura. If our personality is attracted to these stories as a solution to the problem of being a person, it's not surprising that they are very seductive.

They are very seductive but they have nothing to do with liberation. This may be one reason why the seeing of liberation can be such a shock. Instead of permanent bliss, great insight or magical powers, it is simply seen that 'I' am empty. What is here is empty space. This may also be why the shock is sometimes accompanied by laughter, when it is realised that all of our labours on the spiritual path had no meaning. It may be seen as a joke, a joke we played on ourselves, or rather a joke that Oneness played on itself.

Oneness pretends to be an individual who thinks it can do something to discover that it is false. Then it is seen that there never was anyone who could crack the code, who could discover the secret.

There never was an individual. There never was separation. There never was autonomy and choice. Seeing this can produce a lot of laughter. Seeing this can reveal everything as a miracle and give rise to gratitude.

It's the very existence of the person that prevents this from being seen as a miracle. It's the existence of somebody that stops this being seen as a miracle by nobody.

When there's somebody here looking for a miracle, it can't be seen as a miracle. When there's nobody here to see that this is a miracle, it's seen as a miracle.

Is the body of any advantage or significance in seeking liberation?

You can't seek liberation without a body. Without a body, there's just Oneness. With a body, there may be Oneness pretending not to be Oneness and seeking Oneness. In other words, the game requires a body.

So the body isn't a problem?

No. But it's often seen as a problem on many religious and spiritual paths. Sometimes it's seen as a gross problem and sometimes as a very refined or subtle problem.

On the gross level, the body may be seen as a problem because it has lusts and desires which are thought to be not of the spirit. So the flesh must be mortified. Join Opus Dei, wear a barbed garter, whip yourself daily, starve yourself, wear a hair shirt. For us to see God we must be scourged of our impure desires.

On the more refined level, the body may be seen as an impediment because it has energetic blocks. So the body must be purified. Clear your chakras, cleanse your aura, prevent the seeds of karma growing, purify your etheric body. For us to become enlightened we must be cleansed of our samskaras.

If someone had been practising meditation or mindfulness for a long time and then liberation was seen, would they stop their practices or continue them?

There are no rules. If there were rules, liberation would not embrace everything and we would be back in duality. There would be liberation over here and whatever the rules excluded from liberation over there.

If the person had been practising meditation because they enjoyed it, there's no reason why the character shouldn't continue meditation when liberation was seen. But if the person hadn't enjoyed meditating but had been gritting their teeth and doing it because of a belief that it would get them somewhere called personal enlightenment, it's likely that both the belief and the practice would fall away when the person was seen through.

Can somebody's personal behaviour tell us anything about whether there has been awakening or liberation?

No, because liberation is completely impersonal.

Certain kinds of behaviour, particularly if they seem ascetic and detached, may be very appealing to some of us who become interested in the idea of enlightenment. But how they are seen always depends on our point of view. For example, there may be a monk who has been practising celibacy for thirty years. We may regard that as indicative of a very high state of spiritual attainment. On the other hand we may regard it as evidence of a disordered personality, an extreme pathological flight from the company of women. Depending on our attitude, we may see the same behaviour as indicating either a profound state of spiritual advancement or a deep state of psychological disturbance.

If we are inclined to make a connection between certain kinds of harmonious behaviour and an elevated spiritual state, we may be impressed by a monk's or a nun's demeanour. We may not be aware that monastics are under instruction to behave in certain ways and not in others. There is usually a strenuous imposition of discipline on a monk or a nun always to behave calmly and serenely. Karen Armstrong's autobiographical account of her training as a nun is very revealing in this way. It is quite clear from her description that you can have no idea from a nun's demeanour what is actually going on beneath the skull – or the habit. The gentle look and the downcast eyes may conceal a furious rage.

Or in the monastic, the persona may be exaggerated and the shadow may be banished to a very unhealthy extent.

As long as we believe that liberation is personal, it seems obvious to us that we should look for signs of it in the behaviour of the guru, the teacher, the wandering ascetic, the monk. They should behave impeccably and we should cast them aside if we learn that they are rogering their devotees or drinking large quantities of vodka. But once liberation is seen, it is known that it is completely impersonal and none of this applies. Nothing that has been said here this afternoon about Oneness has anything to do with me, my character or my behaviour, except that the flavour of the communication is somewhat determined by the character.

****

I have a real problem when you say there's no time or space.

I'm not surprised.

It's obvious to me that there's both. Take space for example. It's clear to me that I came here from my home and that I'll go back there tonight after this talk is over. There is a city outside this room. There's a street waiting for me to step into it. So in what way do you mean it when you say that there isn't any space?

I mean it literally.

Having said that, I'd add that this has no importance. It doesn't matter because it makes no difference. What are you going to do with it? I'll take a bet that your home, although it doesn't exist, will arise at an appropriate time, which also doesn't exist.

Apart from that, all I can say is that "There's no time or space" is a description of what's seen in liberation. The mind can never make any sense of that. Nevertheless, this is it. This is all there is in its entirety.

There is a city outside this room, but it exists only as an idea which is being discussed by you and me.

What is 'real' is whatever phenomena are arising in this. The thought that there is a city outside this room is a real thought.

This is not just a challenge to a person, it's impossible for a person to understand.

Let us say that sitting here speaking these words there is a character. Does that character live in time and space? Yes, Richard the character lives in time and space. Richard, sitting here, has a memory of having breakfast in a café a couple of hours ago.

Richard does not have a mind and neither do you. Nevertheless, all the manifestations that we think of as belonging to a mind, thoughts, perceptions, sensations and feelings, go on here. These phenomena can only happen in time. As this character has thoughts and perceptions, this character lives in time. It would be more accurate to say that this character lives in the illusion of time or in the appearance of time. Yet it is seen that this is all there is and this is timeless. It is seen impersonally and not by the character that there is no such thing as time. Therefore there is no such thing as a couple of hours ago when the character thinks he had breakfast.

Thank you. That was fantastic. I didn't understand a word of it but it was fantastic. (Laughter)

Can I quote that on the back of my next book? "I didn't understand a word of it but it was fantastic."

4

Love Dreams Differences
Where There Are None

We're here to talk about non-duality. We're here to talk about Being, Oneness. What a way to spend a Saturday afternoon. We could be out shopping.

We could say that liberation doesn't even exist or we could equally say that liberation is already everything. We might wonder what the point is of exploring this at all and yet somehow here we are.

What comes to me as a starting point are some of the ways that we try to make sense of this mystery. There has been a series of programmes on television recently about healers. The last one was about a healer called Ray, a very down to earth chap. He was once a plumber or something like that. He now drives from place to place in a mobile home with his wife and has an extensive healing practice. Lots of people come to him, except that it isn't Ray who does the healing. Ray vacates his body, which is then taken over by Saint Paul.

Who?

Saint Paul. The one and only Saint Paul. Ray vacates his body and Saint Paul takes it over. Saint Paul was from an area which is now in Turkey but for some reason he speaks with an upper-middle-class English accent. He's very unlike Ray. He's much better spoken.

Ray's daughter talked about how she doesn't get to see much of her father because he spends so much time being taken over by Saint Paul. She seemed quite sad about this and so she came along to a healing session to meet Saint Paul for the first time. There was a strange scene where she was introduced to what was physically her father, but of course he didn't recognise her because he was Saint Paul who had never met her before. They had a rather strained conversation and then Saint Paul left Ray's body and Ray came back. He seemed rather surprised to find his daughter there.

In a way this is a very sweet story. It's such a lovely example of the ways that we make sense of our lives as people and give our lives purpose and meaning. Ray and his wife seemed very happy because they had found this meaningful work and could drive from place to place in their mobile home. They seemed very sincere.

We tell wonderful stories to give our lives purpose. We tell very colourful stories, both as individuals and in groups. The group stories are often known as religions.

There is such a powerful, fundamental need to make sense of this. We are born, we become self-conscious and in becoming self-conscious we take on the identity of a person. The person feels separate, the person feels vulnerable and dissatisfied. Most of all, the person feels that there's something missing. So here we are trying to make sense of something which is a total mystery. The ways in which we try to make sense of it are legion. They can range from the most sublime such as "I have dedicated myself to the service of humanity through healing" to the most banal, such as "I have dedicated myself to going shopping." Not that there's anything wrong with going shopping.

Can we go now? (Laughter)

Yes, you've paid, so you can go now.

Many of us find enormous comfort in the stories that we tell. In a way we could be considered very fortunate if a religious story appeals to us because then our purpose for being on the planet, our sense of meaning, is clear. A religion also gives us a community, the company of like-minded people. Or the story that appeals to us might be one about political or social action, about striving to make the world a better place.

But what can happen is that at a certain point all of this can fail us, whether it's Catholicism, or angel channelling, or socialism, or healing through Saint Paul, or shopping.

Whatever the meaning is that sustains us, ultimately we may plunge into the dark night of the soul. Our sense of meaning may disappear but the sense of being a person may stay with us. Now we may really be in trouble because what this can leave us with is existential despair.

The existential problem can be summed up in the following way. We are born and then we die and these two circumstances are not problematic in a fundamental way. They might seem problematic, but in an important sense they are not, because they take care of themselves. Nobody has to do anything about getting themselves born or dying. These two events just happen. But for a person there is of course a space in between birth and death called time, however long that may be. Perhaps three score years and ten. The existential problem lies in that space between birth and death, which somehow has to be structured or filled. It seems to a person that something has to be done with it and that this 'something' should be meaningful. But when we run out of meaning, or meaning abandons us, we're in trouble.

I was at a talk on Buddhism recently given by an elderly professor who used to be a Methodist minister. He was the last Methodist ever to be officially tried for heresy. This was in the early nineteen seventies. He was found guilty and was told "Four hundred years ago we'd have been able to burn you." Apparently he had been writing his sermon one day when he realised that he didn't believe in God any more. Atheism had sneaked up on him.

This is an example of how meaning can sustain us for a while and then not sustain us any longer. If the person is still there, which it usually is, we are then left looking into the existential void. We are faced with the question "What happens now?" We are left with all this time which still has to be structured. "I am a person and I've got to do something with this time that remains."

Not everybody can face this. Some people kill themselves if the existential dilemma becomes intense enough. Sometimes it's that serious.

This is the dilemma that faces us when our sense of meaning drops away. Often we deal with this by simply finding another meaning. We give up Catholicism and become a Buddhist. Eventually, nevertheless, meaning might run out altogether and leave us in despair.

But we're here to talk about the other possibility. Instead of meaning dropping away, the person can drop away. When the person drops away, that doesn't tend to leave existential despair, because then it's seen that there never was that kind of a problem. There never was a person who ever had to do anything to fill time. There is no time to fill and there is no one who could fill it.

The sense of meaning is centred around our having a core sense of choice. We choose to find this meaningful but we don't choose to find that meaningful. We choose to find the Pope meaningful but we don't choose to find the Ayatollah meaningful. Or we choose to find gambling meaningful but we don't choose to find Buddhism meaningful. It's a serious business. We have these choices to make and we'd better make sure we pick the right one because, in some stories, we risk ending up in hell-fire if we make the wrong one. It's a real catastrophe if we chose gambling when we should have chosen Catholicism. We'll have an eternity of hell-fire to repent that in.

When the person falls away, all of this is seen through and so all the stories drop away as well. They are seen simply as stories so they can no longer be taken seriously.

Of course they can still be taken as entertainment. There may still be a delight in the story, but only as entertainment. The character who is left when the person falls away may still enjoy going to Catholic mass but the meaningfulness of that will be seen through. That's a fundamental part of this description of liberation, a defining characteristic of it, that the stories are necessarily seen through. They cannot be taken seriously any more but they may still be enjoyed.

Very often when the person falls away, the stories are no longer enjoyed and so they are simply given up. There may be a tendency for the character to stop going to mass or following their guru or attending chakra cleansing workshops. But there's no necessity for this to happen. The character may continue to enjoy all of those things and go on doing them for the colour, the ritual, the magical feeling, the creativity of them and perhaps most of all for the company, the company of what used to be like-minded friends and are now perhaps simply friends.

You say the person falls away and the stories are seen through. Can we also say that everything is seen as story?

Yes. Paradoxically, all that's left is story. And what we're talking about here is also a story, the story of non-duality. Let's make no mistake about that. We can't use words about anything without spinning a story. But non-duality is the story which points as directly as possible to what actually is, whereas most stories spin imaginative complexities on top of what is.

Of course the stories that are being spun are also 'what is'. The story of Catholicism or of Buddhism may also be what is arising at times. But in any other sense, these other stories complicate the absolute simplicity of this. We tell these stories with all their complications because a person often cannot bear the simplicity of this. For a person, with all our hopes and fears and sense of vulnerability and dissatisfaction and our overwhelming sense that "This isn't it", the simplicity of this often isn't enough. It's boring or it's unsatisfying or it's scary or it makes us angry or sad and we feel a need to change it. So we tell these other stories, we spin these wonderful acts of the imagination.

When the person drops away, it is realised not only that this is always all there is, but that this is sufficient. That's why searching stops, because this is seen to be already fascinating enough in its simplicity.

If a healer can psychically empty themselves and be taken over by another personality, does it mean they are more awakened or enlightened than an ordinary person?

No. It's an experience. No experience has any more or any less to do with liberation than any other experience, whether it's drinking a cup of tea or healing someone's arthritis. In liberation the simplicity of drinking a cup of tea is sufficient but healing may still arise. If the person was healing before liberation, the character might go on healing afterwards. But it will no longer be seen as giving purpose and meaning to life because there's no need for that anymore. However, healers do not all give up healing and drink tea instead when liberation is seen. And being a healer has no more relevance to liberation than having a doctorate in mathematics or being a taxi driver.

Richard, how do you know you're not kidding yourself?

(Laughing) Because there is no one. Who is there to kid or be kidded?

The mind?

There is no mind. There is only a thought. When this is seen, it is known that there is no mind. So who is there to kid or be kidded and what does it matter anyway? What would it matter if I were a complete fake? How would it matter if this was all nonsense and I was making it up? That could only matter to a person who felt that they had something to gain from being here.

There is nothing to be gained from being here. I mean that in both ways. There is also Nothing to be gained from being here. You have to pay double if you gain Nothing from being here. *(Laughter)*

60

So if I were a fake, it could only matter as a story. "I paid ten quid and went to a lot of effort to go and see that bloke, and you know what? He's a complete charlatan! Either that or he's totally self-deluded!"

How do you know you're not self-deluded?

Because there's no one here to be self-deluded.

Because of what you've seen?

No. Because of what has been seen. I haven't seen anything because there's no 'I' to see it. And you won't see this either but it might be seen when you're not there. So there's no one here to delude himself.

But this answer isn't likely to satisfy the mind. Your mind will make of it whatever it wants to. I'm using purposive language, but another way of putting this is there will simply be whatever thoughts arise about what is said here. At some point it might be seen that there is no mind from which they are arising. Thoughts just arise out of emptiness. There is no thinker just as there is no doer.

What can I do to get rid of the mind?

You can't get rid of the mind, partly because there's no mind and partly because there's no you.

But at the moment it feels like I'm holding onto my mind.

Yes, that's what it sometimes feels like to a person.

What would it be like to have nothing to hold onto? It sounds scary to me.

Just being with nothing to hold onto. Just being happening. But you can't get rid of the mind. The sense of you is an illusion and

61

so is the sense of a mind. An illusion cannot do anything. But if 'you' drop away, what is discovered is that there isn't any need for anything to hold on to.

The stories are something to hold on to. They're strap handles. It's as if we're standing in a train that's rattling about and it's really uncomfortable. So we need strap handles to hang on to; Christianity here and Islam there and "I'm an alcoholic" over there and "I'm a humble servant of the Lord and I do good works for mankind" over there. They're all strap handles that we need to hold on to, because being a person can be really scary. When the person drops away there's no need to hold on to anything any more. That's why all the stories are seen through. We don't need to hang on to the stories because now we're in free-fall in being. When it's seen that I no longer do anything, that I'm no longer in control of my life because I no longer have a life, then there's just being. There's just drinking tea. Or just saving the planet. It doesn't matter which. Saving the planet is also good. But it's just what's happening.

There's no need to worry about what will happen if you're no longer there. Everything takes care of itself. Life goes on. What's more, it's seen that this was actually always the case. Life was always just happening. Forget every choice that you may think you have made in your life. There was never a 'you' that made any of those choices. So if liberation is seen, free floating existence in being is not a problem.

All our achievements gone. All those books we wrote or the companies we ran or the elections we won – there was never anybody who did any of that. It just happened.

We have a constant wish to have a centre to refer to. But really there are just ideas balancing against each other, so-called knowledge piled up in books that refer to other books. We can't find a centre. All the ideas are man-made. They're necessary for the world to function, but actually they're just collections of images. What is there to replace the non-existent centre?

Free-falling in mystery. Free-falling through mystery.

A person has a crucial need for stories, for purpose, for meaning. We put enormous energy into creating them. First we create them as ideas but they're not solid enough for us so we have to turn them into buildings. We build churches and temples and then we go to war in order to maintain our story over other people's stories. We slaughter people who have a different story. It's incredible what the energy of these stories creates. There is an absolute need to believe in something. "There is purpose and I've discovered what it is." We don't just invent a religion. We then have to build the Vatican or the Shwe Dagon Pagoda to sustain it.

Whenever somebody has spoken clearly about liberation, after they're dead we might as well forget about what they actually said. If they managed to get people to listen to them, within two hundred years there might be another religion. And it will have little to do with what they said. There's such a resistance to hearing this simple communication. "This is it? Well, I'm sorry – if this is it, it isn't enough!"

We build empires around these stories about crucifixions and ancient prophets of the Lord and elephant-headed gods. These stories are all works of the imagination, some of them very beautiful works of the imagination.

We acquire an understanding of who we are in relation to others through these stories in our culture.

If we look at what a person is as a psychological and emotional organism, it goes beyond that. There is a need to make sense out of what seems senseless, to find purpose in what seems purposeless and to bring comfort to this wounded feeling of dissatisfaction and separation.

Isn't it a need to understand something beyond everyday experience?

These stories arise because in becoming a person, which means in becoming self-conscious, we know we've lost something. Even when things seem pretty good we know that there's something missing, there's something else to get. That's why we have a sense that this isn't it. It might almost be it, but it isn't it. And so we look for something else rather than noticing the wonder of this.

What's been lost is the sense of unity. The sense of unity into which we are born is inevitably lost as soon as self-consciousness arises. Self-consciousness is consciousness of myself as being separate from everything else.

Are there people who've never felt separate, who've never lost the sense of Oneness?

There are a few people who report that they have never really had that sense of being a separate person. But they are exceptions. For most of us self-consciousness arises, separation arises and the sense of a person arises. Then life becomes a problem, even when it's going well.

Is Oneness the same as fullness?

It's possible for Oneness to be seen without fullness being seen. That's what I describe as awakening. The sense of being a person falls away so what is seen is Oneness, but it's an empty Oneness. The fullness of the void isn't seen but that can't be realised at the time.

Awakening can be staggering, so when the person comes back afterwards they may be inclined to think "Wow! There can't be anything else but that! Now how can I scramble my way back to it?" Here, it was only later that the fullness of Oneness was seen.

I'm trying to match what you're saying to spiritual experiences that have happened here.

I was searching for thirty years through spiritual and psycho-therapeutic practices. The spiritual practices brought transcendent experiences which were thought to have something to do with approaching nearer to enlightenment, because I'd read a lot of stories about that. It's difficult to describe transcendent experiences but it's not impossible. For me they had a kind of evanescent quality where the boundaries of the person softened and expanded. The person who might be angry in the kitchen when he opened his tax demand usually became much softer on a meditation retreat. It was only when the person dropped away for a split second that it was seen that these experiences had nothing to do with awakening because awakening is not an experience. There is no one there in awakening to have an experience.

Awakening is a paradigm shift. It has nothing to do with experiences of any kind. The paradigm shift is from somebody walking down a road, for example, to there just being walking down a road but no one doing it.

Awakening is an energy shift and there seem to be some common characteristics in its aftermath. Even though the person comes back, their perception tends to be changed. For example, time tends to be seen through after awakening. The energy that the person had bound up with the meaning of the past and the meaning of the future tends to dissipate.

So is there still affect after this? Is there still joy and other feelings?

Yes, of course. Wouldn't it be awful otherwise?

From what you're saying, that's not the way it's coming across.

(*Laughing*) How's it coming across? As a sort of joyless muddy gloom?

You're talking about 'seeing through the stories' and 'dropping the sense of self'. Where's the life in it?

Where's the juiciness? You could say that things become more juicy when liberation is seen because there's a tendency for some neurosis to drop away. From a psychological and emotional point of view, neurosis gets in the way of juiciness. The more neurosis manifests, the less availability there is for the enjoyment of life.

In liberation, life may be more full-on because there is no longer a neurotic person getting in the way and filtering out experience.

There are certain natural feelings that simply bubble up out of nothingness, for example, anger, sadness, fear and joy. These not only continue to bubble up but they are likely to do so more strongly. But neurotic feelings might lessen or die away. The attenuated neurotic versions of natural feelings, like a habit of irritation, might die away and what might be left could be a more juicy anger rather than the less juicy irritation that was experienced before. The psycho-physical organism is able to hang on to neurotic feelings for a long time, so we can stay irritable or anxious for many months or even years. People can sometimes sulk for years. Sulking is a neurotic or attenuated form of anger. In liberation this tends to end, although there is no necessity for that to happen.

What can be left instead may be the richness of natural feelings that simply continue to arise. Neurosis is also a great destroyer of joy. A neurotic personality will often turn joy into anxiety. In situations where a non-neurotic personality might experience joy, a neurotic personality will often experience anxiety instead. If that neurotic personality falls away, there may be a more open psycho-physical organism remaining, which may be more available to feeling joy.

Doesn't neurosis enrich us? For some of us, isn't it a spur to our creativity? Without neurosis we wouldn't have a lot of our great art and literature.

Neurosis contributes a great deal to the arts in the West. We might think that if we didn't have neurosis, we wouldn't have Dostoevsky, we wouldn't have Tchaikovsky, and that would be a terrible loss. Art as therapy can obviously be highly creative. But creativity doesn't require neurosis. Creativity simply expresses itself in certain ways if it's expressed through a neurotic personality and in different ways if it isn't.

We don't need to worry about losing our wonderful neurotic art, because it isn't going to happen. The population is not going to wake up en masse tomorrow to find it's not there. So the story of neurotic art, without which we wouldn't have 'Crime and Punishment' or 'Swan Lake', isn't going to stop.

I used to think it was worth improving my state of mind, but pain and suffering just seem to go on. So I don't see much point in becoming less neurotic or less angry.

I am saying that if liberation is seen, neurosis might drop away. I'm not saying that if we get rid of our neurosis, liberation will be seen.

But if a person feels themself to be uncomfortable in a prison and believes that they can do something about this, it can be very effective for them to deal with their neurosis through psychotherapy or meditation for example. Alcohol is also very good in the short term, but it does far more liver damage so I don't recommend it. *(Laughter)*

But none of this has anything to do with what we're talking about here. Dealing with my issues with my mother and my father or beating out my anger on a cushion makes no difference to the seeing of liberation.

****

If liberation is seen, all sorts of things stay the same, like memories. So what actually does change?

The sense that there is someone. That disappears. The energy bound up with memory also tends to dissipate so although memories remain, there is less impulse to access them and they're seen through. That means that they're seen for what they are, as thoughts arising in this about an imaginary time in an imaginary life.

That's very helpful.

(Laughing) I can't think how. The last thing I want to do here is be helpful.

There is an identification with the body, with pain for example, isn't there? There is a sense that "This is what I am."

When the person is seen through there's no identification with the body, there's just the body. If the knee hurts, it hurts. That doesn't change. A headache is still a headache, but there's no one having it.

The body-mind organism still protects itself. If we get too close to a flame, we'll flinch away

What about the jivanmukta, the fully realised man? And to what extent is the body essential for liberation?

It's not remotely essential because there is no liberation. Or to put it the other way round, there is only liberation. There's a body-mind organism, which is why this appears to be happening, but it doesn't matter. It's totally inessential, except that if there wasn't a body-mind organism, this wouldn't be happening and we wouldn't be going to have tea soon.

You get many wonderful stories about fully enlightened beings in the Yogic tradition and in other traditions. Sometimes these stories are about detachment. It's perfectly possible to practise techniques which will produce this and some people have a predilection for detachment in any case. One of the problems with detachment is that it tends not to be very juicy. But if I'm desperately looking for spiritual wisdom and I find a person who seems very detached, I may think "He's got something spiritual because he's not affected by the world."

Of course he's not affected by the world because he's detached. So what? All this means is that he's detached, it doesn't mean anything else. But this can seem very attractive, especially to men. Or rather, I should say that whether we're a man or a woman, it can be very appealing to the part of each of us which is more masculine. There can be a masculine drive to stay away from the fire of the emotions because it burns us and the way to do that is to become detached.

A spiritual seeker may see something magical and spiritual in this. But it has nothing to do with either magic or spirituality. It's just detachment.

Detachment often arises out of a lot of neurosis. The person gets fed up with their neurosis so they deal with it by becoming detached. You can do a variety of meditation practices that will produce this. In fact you can practically guarantee that if you do any meditation practice for several hours a day, it will produce it. But there's no juice to it, there's no life to it. Catherine Ingram writes about how she practised Buddhism very assiduously for seventeen years and developed a high degree of detachment. Then she realised it had nothing to do with liberation and she gave it up.

Mind you, you might just as well spend seventeen years developing detachment as go horse racing for seventeen years.

Horse racing may be more expensive. (Laughter)

It depends which horses you back or which guru you practise your detachment with.

****

Is there a way of bringing the seeker closer to understanding liberation?

The seeker can get closer to understanding this conceptually in all sorts of ways but that has nothing to do with seeing liberation, seeing an end to separateness. The mind is always looking for something which it thinks will bring it closer, any little hook which it can use to attach itself to this. "I know he said there's nothing you can do, but he's just hinted that if you watch the gap between your thoughts, it might get you somewhere." Because the mind functions on understanding, one of the biggest hooks is "If I can understand this, somehow it will be seen. Perhaps if I read lots of books about it, then I will get it."

The mind really loves complexity. So if the mind has understood the simple things about this, it will look for more and more complex ideas and spin ever more complicated stories about it. So from the simplicity of non-separation, the mind will give rise to thirty-seven different levels of enlightenment and the hundred and eight techniques which will help us to reach them. These concepts become more and more complex as new minds add new complications to them.

As soon as we move away from the simplicity of just describing this, we tend to move into stories. These are often very articulate, very persuasive and very seductive stories. Usually they are about things which we can do, about techniques which we can practise. But the person who is telling us to do them often did not do them himself. The mind seduces itself into thinking there are helpful processes, even when it is obvious that the person giving us the practices didn't practise them. For example, someone who was deep in depression and then suddenly awakened may tell us to watch the gaps in our thoughts. But that is not how he awakened.

Are there certain techniques or certain experiences that facilitate this seeing? Some people suggest listening to particular pieces of music, others suggest breathing techniques for example. Is there anything wrong with that?

There's nothing wrong with it, but it's misleading because none of that has anything to do with seeing liberation. But it doesn't matter. It's just as divine to mislead people as not to mislead them.

There's nothing wrong with any practice. In the story of a person who is unhappy and feels they can make choices, many of them are very effective. Mindfulness for example can be a very effective way of reducing the level of suffering in our personal prison. That is why it is used now in mental health services. But it has nothing to do with what we're talking about here. Listening to music is wonderful but it has nothing to do with this. There is nothing the person can do to bring about their own disappearance. There's nothing that the false self can do to realise that it is itself false.

When you judge that someone is saying something that is misleading, you're still dabbling in duality.

'Misleading' is a judgemental word. I am a judgemental character so I quite like using such terms. But if you want to avoid the word 'misleading' because it is judgemental, you could say instead that some descriptions point directly to this, some point indirectly to it, and some point in the opposite direction. The suggestion that there is somebody who can use a technique to bring about the seeing that they are nobody is definitely pointing in the opposite direction. It doesn't matter, but it is.

But it's no better to point towards it.

That's right. It's no better or worse to point in one direction or the other. Some people are attracted to one direction, some to the other and it doesn't matter which.

It does to me though!

It does if there's a person to whom it matters.

In the world of dualism I've come here to listen to you pointing towards this. If somebody else was here pointing in a different direction, that wouldn't be o.k.

Not for that character sitting there.

So in the world of dualism that I live in, it does really matter.

Yes, it does for the person. There's a person there who prefers this, rather than wanting me to come in here and hand out mantras. But there'll be another person somewhere who really wouldn't like this meeting simply because it's not in a pub. For a person, any aspect of the story may be important. When the person drops away, it's seen that it isn't.

This character has taught meditation and other transpersonal techniques. Now I prefer to talk about this instead. But it doesn't matter.

What about the body? There's always the presence of the body.

Not if the body dies, there isn't. Maybe you have an assumption that it's important that liberation is seen while there's a body-mind around. It's not important. You can't fail at this, or rather this can't be failed at.

L Ron Hubbard famously said "Give me a revolver and I'll liberate anybody."

Yes, others have said "The only way I could liberate you is to shoot you."
    L Ron Hubbard spent the last ten years of his life at sea. He had a yacht where girls in camp sailors' outfits attended to his every whim. Not bad, eh? If you're going to be a guru, you might as well have the fringe benefits. *(Laughter)*

If I don't get my moment of liberation ...

You will never get it. That's the bad news. Nevertheless it cannot help but be got. That's one hundred per cent decisive, but not necessarily while the psycho-physical organism is still around to notice it. And it doesn't matter. Being awake and being asleep are the same. It's just that if I'm asleep, that can't be seen.

What about the ego? It's very tied up in the story.

When the person drops away the ego is seen to be just another thought and all the stories are seen through. Whether it's the story of the opening of the thousand-petalled lotus chakra or the story of cardinals rushing around the Vatican in important red hats, it's seen through. It's seen to be about nothing. It's not a bit about something. It's not partly real. "It's a tale ... full of sound and fury, signifying nothing."

I feel there have been glimpses of this and I've felt a real fear because of it.

That fear may be evoked by the sense that the straps we've been hanging onto aren't really there. Even a hint of this could evoke fear. Imagine, if we've been brought up as a Roman Catholic with the story of guilt and hell-fire, and that starts to drop away. We start to suspect that we're hanging on to an imaginary strap. That could evoke fear. Suddenly we might lose our bearings, lose all the fixed points in our life and then even plunge into terror.

But fear is also a natural emotion, like anger, sadness and joy. Natural emotions simply come up. The mind thinks there must be a reason but they can simply come up at times.

In one of its deepest insights, psychotherapy sometimes gets quite close to non-duality when it recognises that the best thing a person can do with fear or with any other uncomfortable emotion is simply to allow it to be felt. Of course in psychotherapy there's the concept of a person who can make a choice to do that, so the comparison with non-duality breaks down at that point. There is a saying within Humanistic Psychology, "The fastest way to freedom is to feel your feelings." That's both close to what we're talking about and a long way away from it. It's a long way away because it holds that there is a person who can make a choice to feel their feelings. So I would say instead that it is simply noticed that sometimes when feelings come up for a person, there's no resistance to them. When that happens those feelings move through the psycho-physical organism at their fastest and cause the fewest problems.

Can the psychotherapist help this by discovering the root of the problem, by discovering where the problem stems from in the person's life?

No. The root of the problem is the sense of being a person. If the psychotherapist believes in the person, which most do, they won't see this. But if you're lucky enough to have a psychotherapist who isn't there, they can go to the root of the problem in a way. There will be a seeing of the root of the problem but there'll also be a seeing that there's nothing that can be done about it. Nevertheless a sharing about it might take place and the client might find that comforting.

If you're seeking a psychotherapist, I'd always recommend a psychotherapist who isn't there. But I don't know how you find them.

In life-threatening situations, people sometimes find that their fear disappears. But when the situation becomes normal again they find their fear returns.

That's simply a survival mechanism. In a situation in which the psycho-physical organism is threatened with extinction, it's not very useful to become paralysed with fear and let the sabre-tooth tiger eat us. It's much more useful if, as people sometimes report, a great calm descends on us while we deal with the threat and wrestle the sabre-tooth tiger to the ground.

****

Do you have to have a strong sense of the self in the first place in order to shed it?

No, it's irrelevant.

But if you don't have this strong sense, how can you shed it?

If you haven't got it, you don't need to shed it. We mentioned earlier that occasionally there are people for whom that sense of being separate never seemed to be there.

If you're suggesting that to see this you need a particular kind of strong egoic structure, no. It's irrelevant. One way of putting this is that you are already totally adequate. There is nothing that you need to do. Indeed, there is nothing that you can do or anyone who can do anything. This is the opposite to what spiritual paths suggest. Spiritual paths imply that you are currently inadequate and you need to do something to become worthy of this great gift. No. There is nothing that needs to be done. You are not deprived of the seeing of liberation because you haven't worked through your bad karma, cleansed your chakras or meditated enough, or because you are not a good enough person or you don't have a strong enough sense of self. There's no one who is inadequate. A sense of inadequacy may arise but it's meaningless.

We are both so much less and so much more than we think we are. We are being itself, in which everything appears including the person. But as a person, we are so much less than a three-dimensional autonomous being. We are the two-dimensional character on the cinema screen. We are like Rick in 'Casablanca', who clearly has no autonomy whatever but who jerks around like a puppet according to the piece of celluloid running though the projector. If we push this metaphor further, we could say that as being we are also the screen, the projector, the celluloid, the lens, the light going through the lens, the auditorium. But as an individual person we don't feel ourself to be that. That may be why we might pump ourself up with grandiosity as a person – perhaps there is a sneaking suspicion that really we are just that two-dimensional play of light. Out of the fear this might evoke may come the grandiosity that means that as a person we need to become the dictator of a Latin American country to make ourself feel ok.

Is that connected to what happens when you start to see things that you've known before as three-dimensional as if they're two-dimensional, as flat rather than 3D? Is that something that's externalised from the inside or are you actually saying that the world is two-dimensional?

It's all externalised from the inside. That's a story too but it's as close as we can get to answering that question.

Does nothing external exist? Is it created by the psycho-physical organism?

You could say that the psycho-physical organism is like the lens in a projector. Or we could say it's like a prism. The undifferentiated white light of being enters the prism of the individual and out come the rainbow colours of this wonderful manifestation. The psycho-physical organism is the lens which produces the appearance of difference, of separation. Of course this sounds very dualistic, so please remember it's a metaphor. It's another story because none of this is actually happening. It's just a way of trying to understand what we're talking about.

A friend of mine has written a book title. We're waiting to see whether a book follows. It might or it might not, but the title is beautiful. It's 'Love Dreams Differences Where There Are None.' You could say that you are the mechanism, or the organism, whereby love dreams those differences where there are none.

Thoughts come up. Sensations come up. Perceptions come up. What is real?

For me, the only sensible way to use the word 'real' is to say that phenomena are real. But they're only real within the dream. If I tell a story with meaning, let's say about personal salvation, my thoughts about it are real phenomena. The story's not real, the story's imaginary, but my imagining of that story, my visualisation of it, my thoughts about it, are all real phenomena.

If I experience myself as channelling angels, the experience of it for me is a real phenomenon. But I'm not channelling angels.

What's that thing on your shoulder? (Laughter)

It's not an angel. It's a parrot. It's my ghostly parrot, a bit of karma left over from a past incarnation as a pirate.

5

Everything Ends In Mystery

Heraclitus, who said that we can never step into the same river twice, also said "Everything ends in mystery." We could add that everything begins in mystery and in the story of time everything also goes on in mystery.

This explains our propensity for telling stories. We are confronted with mystery, with the unexplained and the unexplainable wherever we look. But our minds have a powerful urge to understand, so we spend a lot of our time making up stories to convince ourselves that we really know what's going on. These stories might be about religion, spirituality, quantum physics or many other things. For a while the mind might find a story satisfactory, which will keep it quiet temporarily. It will seem as if we have explained the mystery, through God, or the quantum state, or Atman and Brahman, or the singularity from which the Universe exploded into being. But each explanation simply posits another mystery because the mind can't really understand how the quantum state, a singularity, God or Brahman explains anything ultimately.

Coming to a talk like this, if what is said is really heard, we are inviting the end of everything. We're inviting the end of meaning, the end of purpose and the end of all the stories that we have ever been told and ever believed in.

We start believing in stories at a very young age. As children we are 'story-believing organisms'. It's very easy for our parents to play the terrible trick of persuading us of the reality of Father Christmas, because we are so credulous. We have such a propensity for believing whatever stories we are told when we are young. Often these stories stay with us for the rest of our lives although they may become more sophisticated. If the child grows up to become a Professor of Theology at Oxford, belief in God may become considerably more sophisticated than belief in Santa Claus.

There is neurological research that shows that influences and experiences in childhood are laid down in the physical structures of our brains at an extremely deep level. It is very difficult to change these structures after the age of about seven or eight. The Jesuits are right when they say "Give us the boy till he's seven and we'll give you the man."

If there is awakening and the person falls away, all the stories may fall away as well, including the ones that I've just told about childhood. Then it may be noticed that there never were any meaningful stories, there never was anyone who could do anything, nor was there ever anything that needed to be done. What may be noticed then is that there is just life happening rather than 'me' making life happen. Making life happen as a person can be very tiring. That's why if this is glimpsed for even half a second, there can be a profound sense of relief.

Of course there can be other reactions to seeing even briefly that the person is a fiction. Despair is quite common as well as relief. Despair can arise because of the realisation that all those years of hope and purpose and effort and striving towards resolution had no meaning. Relief can arise if it's also realised that there was never anybody who made any effort, there is no one who needs to make an effort and there is no one who can make an effort.

We are not living life. Life is living us. Life living us is a lot less effort.

The 'me' that thinks that I am living life believes that I am making choices. The simplest choice can be exhausting. For some people the choice "Shall I wear my pink shirt or my white shirt today?" can be exhausting, never mind "Shall I marry Mary or Elizabeth?" or "Shall I become an architect or a doctor?" If that all drops away, there can be a tremendous sense of relief and release and a noticing that this is already a miracle which needs no story. It can be noticed that there is no need to do anything, or go anywhere, to make my life better or to look for a miracle somewhere else because this is already paradise.

Alternatively, there can be a plunge into despair as the meaning of my life is stripped ruthlessly away.

Richard, were you a seeker for long?

Oh yes. I've got medals for seeking – thirty years of conscious seeking through spiritual and psychotherapeutic means. Of course we are all seekers, some of us consciously, some of us unconsciously. We are all seeking to put an end to the sense of dissatisfaction which haunts us even when things are going well. There are many ways of seeking. Going up and down the escalators in department stores all over the country at this moment are many, many seekers. They are seeking to put an end to their sense of dissatisfaction through shopping rather than through meditation or through sitting at the guru's feet.

Seeking is very addictive. These days many of us are very intelligent seekers. We've given up seeking through the old superstitious religious ways of pitting God against the devil. Now our ways of seeking, through psychotherapeutic practices and spiritual techniques for example, can be very effective at producing beneficial changes in our experience. In other words, on the level of the person, they work. They repay the energy that the person puts into them, although they have nothing to do with the seeing of non-duality.

Psychotherapeutic techniques can be very effective at changing the nature of the relationships that a person experiences. That means both our relationships with others and our relationship to ourself. Spiritual practices can also be particularly effective at changing our relationship with ourself.

With spiritual techniques, as long as there is a person here who feels that we are practising them, it is difficult not to see that as moving us towards a spiritual goal. In other words, it is difficult not to buy into the story of spiritual evolution. If we find a guru with whom we feel good and we interpret that as a sign of a transmission of spiritual energy, we are almost bound to feel that this is moving us along a spiritual path towards a goal of final enlightenment. It's a very convincing story. It's only when the person drops away that it can be seen that this is irrelevant. There never was anybody who was inadequate and therefore there never was anybody who needed to move along a spiritual path to anything.

Given the existential problem that there seems to be time between birth and death which needs to be structured, filling some of it with psychotherapeutic and spiritual practices is probably just about the most intelligent thing that a person can do. Even more intelligent than going shopping.

Is liberation living in complete freedom once I am willing to let myself drop away?

Liberation is freedom from the sense of being a person who has a life to live but it is also the seeing that there is no person who makes free choices about anything.

So we could say there is both total freedom and a complete loss of freedom. There is freedom from the burden of being a person, freedom from the sense of having to achieve anything, freedom from the past with its guilts and regrets and freedom from the future with its hopes and expectations. But there is also a complete loss of the freedom to do anything as an autonomous individual, the realisation that rather than *we* being free to do anything, everything is simply being done.

And we need to be careful with your phrase 'once I am willing to let myself drop away' because the seeing of liberation has nothing to do with our willingness. We cannot will liberation or not will it.

But I can let my resistance to liberation go?

Absence of resistance can happen. We can't do anything about that because there is no one here. The idea that we should try very hard to let our resistance go is a part of many spiritual paths. But then we just have a person who is resisting resistance. "If I struggle harder with my resistance, I can force it to drop away!" It's absurd.

It may be the seeing of this absurdity that sometimes produces a lot of laughter when liberation is finally seen. There was never anyone resisting liberation. There was only ever emptiness.

Some teachers set a kind of spiritual homework. "Look inside for the person, the one who experiences all of this." The idea is that no matter how long or how deeply we look inside, we will never find that person because inside there is only emptiness from which everything arises. But this homework won't be useful, because as long as there is the sense of a person looking inside for something, that sense will be there. And when the person drops away, there's no need to do the homework because it simply becomes obvious that there was never any one there.

Where do all the spiritual paths and practices come from?

They come partly from the existential problem, the need to structure the time that apparently exists between birth and death. We can fill it in many ways; for example by going to the betting shop, by shopping, by becoming an alcoholic, by saving the planet or by devoting ourself to a religion. Or we can follow a spiritual path and practise spiritual techniques.

So we could say that following a spiritual path, like becoming an alcoholic, is just one of the ways that we can structure the time that we have on the planet. But following spiritual paths is a much more intelligent way of structuring time, partly because it's quite likely to make us feel better and partly because it's so infinitely colourful and interesting. The next bottle of vodka is pretty much the same as the last bottle of vodka but spiritual paths are so varied. And like religions, they can be made complicated beyond belief. There will always be new material to fill the mind. If we think we've understood the twenty-three levels of enlightenment, we can always find another teacher who says "Well actually, there are twenty-nine."

So spiritual paths provide particularly juicy, wonderful, colourful stories.

In spite of the frustration of all the searching and the many years of following lots of different spiritual paths, and even though it may be seen as useless, it could all be seen as perfect?

Absolutely perfect. And it doesn't matter whether it is or whether it isn't because there's no choice anyway. But that can turn into a method. "I'll throw myself into as many spiritual paths as possible. I'll practise Buddhism and Shamanism and Kriya Yoga. Through that process, I'll realise that none of this actually gets me to see there is no one, so it will all fall away and then I'll see presence."

But there's nobody who can do any of this just as there is nobody who chose to come here today. What happens is simply what happens. Meditating or not meditating, following a guru or not following a guru, clearing my chakras or not clearing my chakras, shopping or not shopping, just happen. So questions about purpose or usefulness can be seen to be irrelevant when it is seen that there is no one who ever had any choice about any of this or who ever did any of this. Nobody has ever meditated or followed a guru or cleared their chakras. Nobody has ever even gone shopping.

But in the story of time, the appearance of all of these things can arise. From the point of view of a person, I'd suggest that it's more intelligent to meditate than to drink vodka.

Spending time in the spiritual supermarkets, doing our spiritual shopping, hopping from one guru to another, is it helpful at all?

No. Nothing is either helpful or unhelpful.

There is a tendency among the more spiritually puritan and stern to condemn guru hopping. "Find yourself a guru, grit your teeth, stiffen your upper lip and stick with it! This frivolous modern generation of long-haired spiritual layabouts can't stick with the same guru for more than ten years before they're off to find another one!"

But for a person, if you become interested in spiritual paths, guru hopping is an intelligent thing to do. Check them out. Try different spiritual techniques. Go to different teachers. Why not? It's like buying a new car – you wouldn't want only to test drive one make. That's not a very intelligent thing to do.

None of this will be helpful or unhelpful. But as long as there's a person, that can't be recognised. A person frequently sits in judgement. Sometimes we sit quite savagely in judgement on other people and we often sit in judgement on ourselves, approving and disapproving of the apparent choices that are being made. Many of us tend to veer from congratulating ourselves to beating ourselves up, from grandiosity to collapse. But none of this is relevant to seeing presence. Nothing has any relevance to seeing presence. That's why it's a bit of a puzzle that we even get together and talk about it.

There are said to be spiritually powerful places like Arunachala, for example. Is it true that some places do have something special about them? Arunachala is so well known. Is it a very powerful and holy place?

In the story, some places have something about them which is different to other places. In addition to that, we tell stories about parts of the story. Many stories are told about Arunachala. And then all of these stories with their beliefs and ideas and feelings and theories accrete around that place. If we know about these, it's likely that when we go to Ramana Maharshi's ashram and walk around that hill we'll think that it's a very wonderful and special experience. Many other places are thought of as special. We don't need to go to India, we could go to Glastonbury Tor. If we are soaked in the right kind of culture, when we go to Glastonbury Tor we will probably experience special feelings and special thoughts that seem to be summoned up by it.

If we want to call these places holy, we will do that. There may be particular kinds of thoughts and feelings which we add on to the physical phenomena associated with these places and which we decide to label 'holy'. These experiences may feel very special but they're also meaningless. Going to the place where Ramana Maharshi had his ashram and walking in his footsteps around the hill is not going to bring us closer to losing ourself. There is no one who could go there and there is no one who could lose themself.

Even if the stories that are associated with these places fall away, there still might be a preference for some places rather than for others. I'd rather spend an afternoon in my local park than on an industrial estate.

Another way of putting this is that everywhere is holy.

The person could fall away even on an industrial estate.

****

Is there any point in being at these talks or is it pointless?

The mind thinks there must be a 'yes' or 'no' answer to that question. The mind says, "It must be one or the other. Either it's useful to be here or it isn't. Come on Richard, which is it?" The frustrating answer to your question is "Neither." Perhaps that only makes sense when it's seen that there is no choice about whether you are at this talk or not and indeed there is no one who is sitting here listening to this talk in any case.

Nothing has ever happened. But you can't expect the mind to make anything of that because it is not equipped to make sense of that statement. The mind lives in time where things appear to happen so it seems obvious to the mind that something is happening every second.

The mind can't imagine nothing happening?

No. The mind, which does not exist as an entity, cannot imagine its own non-existence.

This is why there are so many religious and spiritual stories. Nearly all of these stories justify the continued existence of the mind beyond physical death, because the mind can't bear the thought of its own annihilation. One of the paradoxes of some spiritual stories is that even when they hold that there is no mind, they still turn into stories about how the mind will live, if not forever, at least for long enough to calm our fears about its disappearance. For example, Buddhism is a spiritual philosophy of no self, and yet what evolves within Buddhism are some highly colourful stories about how the 'no self' which doesn't exist is going to continue, and continue developing, at least for many aeons. This is close enough to 'forever' to satisfy the mind. Delaying the contemplation of the mind's annihilation for many aeons is delaying it long enough for most minds.

One of the teachings of the Buddha is that there is nothing that can be said about nirvana. He gave it no characteristics or conditions. Two and a half thousand years later we have forms of Buddhism which hold that there are entire Buddha realms which Buddhas pass on to and where they continue to evolve spiritually. So our almost never-ending individual existence, which is evolving and growing and which can enjoy that evolution virtually forever, continues on and on down countless aeons of time.

So if our elevation to Buddhahood were to occur in five hundred lifetimes, we don't need to worry even then about that being the end of personal identity, because as a Buddha we will simply be reborn into a Buddha realm where we will continue to evolve.

The Buddha's point was very simple but we are very good at missing the point.

At their core, what these intensely colourful and wonderful stories stem from is that there is a person who cannot contemplate their own annihilation. It's both too painful and too unimaginable. But when it's seen that there is no person in any case, this ceases to be a problem.

****

Suffering seems to drive a lot of doing.

Essentially our sense of dissatisfaction, our sense that there is something missing, drives doing or produces a lot of activity. For some of us our dissatisfaction may be about the planet being in a mess, so we throw ourselves into trying to clear some of the mess up. For others, the sense of dissatisfaction may be about our inner state and we're more likely to end up in psychotherapy or on a spiritual path. Or of course we could have psychotherapy, meditate and work to save the planet.

Couldn't we say that suffering doesn't really exist?

The trouble with that is there is a level of reductionism which becomes unhelpful. If there's a bad tooth ache, saying that suffering doesn't exist may not sound very convincing.

I was suggesting in a talk recently that all feelings could be said to come down to some version of anger, fear, sorrow or joy. Someone said "You could say that all the negative feelings just come down to one, which is fear." Someone else said "There's only one core feeling, love. Fear, sorrow and anger are simply an absence of love." In a way you could say that. I'm quite happy to sit here and say "The nature of everything is unconditional love." But it seems to me that this is a level of reductionism which isn't useful. For a person, and if the person drops away this will continue, the feelings of anger, sorrow and fear are likely to arise at times. To reduce that to "There's only one core feeling, love", although true, may not be very helpful.

I thought you've said that there is no help and nothing's any use.

I just mean helpful and useful in terms of understanding. Nothing is going to help us to get anywhere with this. Nothing is useful in that sense.

Is feeling good a better condition to be in than feeling miserable and depressed on this road to liberation?

No. It's no better at all. And we're not on a road to liberation.

Of course it's better in the experience of the person but that has no relevance to liberation. There are accounts of liberation being seen after long and profound periods of depression. Or after long periods of alcoholism. These are not recipes or methods, by the way. *(Laughter)*

Is it possible that there is no reality to karma but we just like to think that it exists?

Yes. It's a story. But it's a particularly juicy and satisfying story. It's so tasty thinking of my boss getting it in the neck in a future life, when I can't give it to him in the neck in this life. It's also juicy to think of myself coming back and getting all the goodness that I deserve. Injustice is an affront to the mind and the story of karma tells us that there will be justice in the end.

To a certain kind of mind, as an explanation of the problem of suffering, karma is much more satisfying and attractive than the explanations that we get from the Abrahamic monotheistic religions. There the answers tend to be some form or other of "God moves in mysterious ways." It's much more logical to suggest that you're suffering now because you behaved like a pig to people in a past life. Or you're going to suffer in the future because you're behaving like a pig to me in this life.

Of course the idea of karma only makes sense when combined with a philosophy of rebirth. It's quite clear that people don't necessarily get their just deserts in this lifetime. So these two ideas go together in a very satisfying way. The mind can be reassured that there has to be rebirth because there's karma to be fulfilled.

This is one of the reasons why so many people are leaving the monotheistic religions and joining the Eastern religions. And why so many people who've never had any interest in the monotheistic religions are now joining the Eastern ones.

The story of karma revolves around an assumption of volition or freely made choices. It makes no sense without this concept. So when volition is seen through, this story drops away.

How important is the nature of the individual story, whether you do well in the story, whether you're happy? Does it have any bearing on liberation?

No. For most people of course, the story of 'me' is supremely important. We are the star in our own movie. We might be a hero or an anti-hero or a humble servant of the Lord, for example. But beyond that, the nature of the story has no importance at all and certainly no relevance to liberation.

****

What is meant by "Except you become as little children you will not enter the Kingdom of Heaven"?

When liberation is seen, there is an innocence about what remains. Because meaning and purpose and striving to reach important goals tend to fall away, what is left is a kind of innocent awareness of life being experienced in immediacy.

But phrased as it is in our translations of the Bible, as is so often the case it is misunderstood. It is expressed as an injunction, as something that you must do in order to be able to enter the kingdom. "You must become as little children first!" In other words, your becoming like a little child is a necessary precursor to you entering the kingdom. But it is not an injunction. It is a description – upon entering the kingdom, you will experience life like a little child once more. In our terms, should the simple seeing of this arise, then what will be left will be an experience which is like the experience of little children. This is because it will be without the interpretations and the meaningfulness and the purposes that the adult mind tends to place on it.

This confusion of effect with cause is very common where spiritual paths are concerned. It is one of the reasons they can become so delusory. For example, if we search in the Himalayas for a holy man and then notice, if we think we've found one, that he seems to have a quiet mind, this is then likely to be misinterpreted as "If I quieten my mind, I will become holy like him." Now you have a technique called 'Quietening The Mind'.

My mind is very troubled. I have lots of very turbulent negative thoughts. Surely that's bad. Is it bad to have thoughts like these?

It's uncomfortable of course. But bad in what sense? Morally bad? Should you be horsewhipped for having an unquiet mind?

Well, I've read that there is the possibility of liberation only in the present moment.

That's because there is only the present, or there is only presence. There's nothing more mysterious or deep about saying that liberation can only be seen in the present than the fact that the present is all there is. There's nothing else to see liberation in. How could liberation be seen in the future or the past? There is no future or past.

But this can be misinterpreted as another injunction. "Be Here Now!" What this really means is "Don't let yourself reminisce or anticipate." For a person it means "Don't think about the past or the future." It's sometimes possible for us not to think about the past or the future for several minutes at a time but this tends to be mentally very constipating.

Of course if there are lots of whirling, noisy, scattered, unpleasant thoughts going on it makes the prison of being a person more uncomfortable. So it's intelligent for the person to try to do something about this, like learning Buddhist mindfulness for example. This can be an excellent way of improving the quality of the experience of a person.

Drinking vodka is another excellent way but it has worse side-effects than Buddhism.

Are you sure? (Laughter)

Perhaps not. Buddhism can have some quite bad side effects as well. It can sometimes produce quite a desiccated personality. Whereas vodka can produce quite a juicy fun personality.

So let's just restrict this to liver damage. I assert that Buddhism causes less liver damage than vodka. *(Laughter)*

Can self-enquiry bring us to the realisation that 'I am that'?

In terms of liberation, self-enquiry doesn't get us anywhere because it is a person who is self-enquiring.

For a person 'I am that' is either just a formula of words or it is an attempt to imagine what it might mean. But a person can't imagine it or understand what it means. The meaning of 'I am that' is revealed only when the person drops away. Then there's the shock of seeing "I am that!"

A person can only philosophise about 'I am that'. It's like the technique of 'Neti, neti', 'Not this, not this'. Seeing that there is no person is as likely to happen when drinking a cup of tea as when contemplating 'I am that' or 'Not this, not this'.

But you can avoid getting caught up in the drama of uncomfortable thoughts that come up for you.

You can't avoid anything. When liberation is seen, uncomfortable thoughts may still arise but there's nobody there taking an interest in them. This is simply a description, but if we think there is cause and effect we may try to practise a technique that goes "When an uncomfortable thought arises, don't invite it in." But we have no choice about whether we invite it in or not because we aren't there. If an uncomfortable thought arises, it will either be invited in or it won't be, but there won't be anybody there giving out the invitation.

So you can't turn this into a technique. Well, it may be turned into a technique but it won't work.

I once had an acquaintance who practised a technique called 'Self-remembering'. It had a rather devastating effect on his personality because he became incredibly boring. When he engaged with you, before each part of the interaction, he had to stop and remember who he really was. He'd come round to see me and I'd say "Hello Jim" and there'd be a pause while he remembered who he really was. Then he'd say "Hello Richard." I'd say "Would you like a cup of tea, Jim?" and he'd pause again to remember who he really was before saying "Yes please, milk and one sugar, Richard." I'd say "Have you been on holiday?" and there'd be another pause while he remembered who he really was. Then he'd say "No, I'm going away next week." This technique made him very bad company.

But there's nothing wrong with self-enquiry. We may look inside and understand that there is no one who is there.

There's nothing wrong with self-enquiry, of course. But this is not about understanding that there's no one there, it's about seeing it. That's just as likely to happen when driving a taxi or drinking vodka as when self-enquiring.

Why are there so many schools of enlightenment with so many techniques?

One reason is that where there is awakening without the seeing that it is an uncaused event, there's often an association made between awakening and whatever the person had previously been doing. The person may lay claim to awakening and say "That was something I achieved." So if the person had previously been meditating for many years, they might set up a School of Enlightenment through Meditation.

Gurdjieff for example seemed to associate awakening with a shocking event. He seemed to think that people could be startled into awakening. So he set up a system where his followers were sometimes subjected to startling unexpected events.

After awakening the person comes back. There are then two possibilities. They will either lay claim to awakening as something they achieved, or they won't. The ones who lay claim to it are likely to found the various schools of 'Enlightenment through

Meditation' or 'Enlightenment through Experiencing Shocks in the Middle of the Night'.

Is the word 'maya' or 'illusion' helpful in understanding this?

The translation of maya as 'illusion' is not very helpful. If I hit my head hard against a wall, there may be concussion and a headache and these won't feel very illusory. I prefer the word 'appearance'. This is an appearance but it seems a very solid one. The metaphor of a dream may also be helpful. When we are in a night-time dream it seems utterly real, utterly convincing. But when we awake, it is clear beyond any doubt that all the things that seemed so real in it, including time, including space and including the presence of a person who seemed to have volition and made purposeful choices, was unreal. I may have dreamt that I drove sixty miles from London to Brighton in two and a half hours but when I wake up in the morning it is clear that neither the sixty miles nor the two and a half hours nor the person doing the driving ever existed. That is a very good metaphor for this.

Can Richard induce the seeing of liberation?

No, because Richard is a fiction. Richard is another thought that arises. It's the same for you, except that added on to the seeing there, may be the sense that there's a person who is doing the seeing.

There is always just seeing. Another way to put this is that there is just being. There is just being over here and there is just being over there, but over there, being may also contain the sense of separation, the sense of a separate person.

There are reports of people losing their sense of self when playing sports, when creating art, when dancing for example.

Awakening is an energy shift. When the person comes back, irrevocable changes may have taken place. When we lose our sense of self in dancing or in playing sport or in art, there may be a parallel, but it doesn't seem to have the same effect of reconfiguring the person. But none of this matters. It's a story. It's stuff happening.

W.B. Yeats summed up the loss of the sense of self beautifully in 'Among School Children':–

> 'O body swayed to music, O brightening glance,
> How can we know the dancer from the dance?'

6

This Is Coming Home

We've come here to talk about a mystery which can't be understood, in words which can't possibly describe it. So let's get started with a solid sense that we're bound to fail. Now we can all relax knowing that failure is certain to be the case.

I've brought a quotation with me which I came across a few days ago. It seemed relevant to me. It's from James Watson, one of the two scientists who discovered the structure of D.N.A. He says "You can say 'Gee, your life must be pretty bleak if you don't think there's a purpose.' But I'm anticipating having a good lunch."

If we really understood that, we could leave now. *(Laughter)*

The other thing that came to me as a starting point arose out of a talk I was giving last month. We were talking about all the blocks that the mind finds in this, all the statements that the mind seems to come up against like a brick wall because they're impossible to really understand. We considered some of these statements: "There's no space." "There's no time." "There's no purpose." "There's no meaning." "There's no choice." Most fundamental of all is "There's no person." There's no one who came here today, there's no today in which they could have come here and there's no here to which this non-existent person could have come. I think I've probably covered all the bases there.

So we really are facing a mystery which is absolutely redolent with paradox. Recently somebody said to me "This all seems rather contradictory." Well, I hope that nothing that is said here is contradictory, but it is extremely paradoxical. And contradiction and paradox may belong not in the same box but in adjacent boxes on the same shelf.

So out of that meeting where we were talking about all these blocks that the mind comes across, I think I may have the title for another book on this, if there's ever to be one. The title could be either 'An Assault on the Mind' or 'An Insult to the Intellect'. This can seem like an insult to the intellect. The intellect says "This is madness! It makes no sense! How can you say that!" And these are all things that my intellect said when I first used to walk up the hill in Hampstead some years ago to listen to Tony Parsons.

(Sound of the front door opening.) Is that someone else arriving?

It might be someone leaving already. (Laughter)

Someone left very early last time, after about fifteen minutes. But someone else got the record for falling asleep after about five minutes so if you're going for that record I'm afraid you've already missed it.

This is a total assault on the intellect. It's like doing violence to the mind. Of course you may not experience it like that. I'm making an assumption. But I used to experience it like that and I talk to people now who express the same feeling. It's almost a violation of the mind. So let's acknowledge that before we plunge deeply into this madness.

Yet in spite of the violence to the intellect and the assault on the mind and the apparent madness of this, here we are. It's as if something in us recognises that this is coming home. This something has nothing to do with the mind or its common-sense rejection of the ideas which are presented here.

For a few of us there is the recognition that this communication goes beyond everything else. It undercuts everything else and makes it irrelevant. Some of us feel this, so as well as thinking "This is absolutely mad. It doesn't make sense", we also sigh with relief because we recognise that sense of coming home.

What that relief may partly be about is that we can begin to allow all of the stories to drop away. Let's acknowledge to start with that everything is story, there is nothing else in the appearance. This is a story, this is a dream. Using a modern metaphor we could say that this is a film. But having acknowledged that everything is story, we can also notice that we enjoy telling stories. We tell them about many things, but perhaps most relevantly to those of us sitting here, we tell them about spiritual paths, religions, meaning and purpose, karma and dharma and related things. The sigh of relief that might be going on for some people may partly be because those stories can now be let go. I could say that it's time for all of them to be let go but that sounds too purposeful. Of course I'm not implying that there is anybody who could let them go. Nevertheless, two of the phenomena that arise here may be a sense of relief and a great big sigh when it is recognised by no one, or by awareness itself, that the stories that we tell are beginning to fall away.

I've discovered a book of poems by Hafiz and one of the poems in it is saying exactly what you've just said.

Ah, he was on the right lines then.

He says "Sit down and take a rest, let your head rest on a cushion, because the hardest work is to be separate." It's such a lovely poem. He's saying you are in extremis, so take a rest. He puts in a poetic way what you've just said.

Yes, it's quite likely that there'd be a long sigh of relief as the head rests on the cushion. What was the phrase about separation?

The hardest work is to be separate.

Yes, for a person. When there's a person who has a sense of separation it doesn't matter what's happening or how well things seem to be going, there'll be the sense that it's still hard work. Because no matter how well things are going, there'll always be a primal sense of dissatisfaction. This will arise out of the fact that as long as there's the sense of a person, there'll be the knowing that there really is a lack, that there really is something missing. I could be driving along in my Mercedes with the top down and my beautiful wife beside me and my lovely children in the back. All of this may be wonderful, but even when life is going as well as it ever possibly could, there will still be a sense of separation and so there can be a sense of dissatisfaction. There can be the feeling that this still isn't it. That may be conscious or it may be sub-conscious. When life's tough, it's really hard. But even when life's going well there can still be the sense that something is missing. I may have no idea what it is because I have forgotten what it was like to be born into a state of unity, to be born into a state where there was only awareness. We could say that 'I' never knew what it was like because there was no self-consciousness when I was born. Nevertheless, from the moment the self-conscious person appeared out of primal awareness, something was lost.

One way of putting this is that the person isn't born at the same time as the baby, the person is born sometime later. The baby is born as a psycho-physical entity but the person isn't born until the sense of being a separate individual arises with self-consciousness. This happens at quite a young age, but not usually at the beginning.

Recently I was talking to someone who said that they could remember the moment of their birth. This was not through any kind of therapeutic process, which is fairly common. They simply remembered it, which is very unusual. But for most of us the self-conscious person isn't born until some time after the birth of the baby. When self-consciousness arises it inevitably gives rise to a sense of separation. You could say they are the same thing. The sense of separation then gives rise to a sense of dissatisfaction with a great deal of what is perceived to be the case. There is a sense of dissatisfaction with many of the phenomena that arise after that because there's a sense that 'I', a person who now feels myself to be separate, have lost something. And I feel this because I *have* lost something. In the gaining of 'me', what has been lost is the sense of unity, the sense of non-separation.

But in order to lose the sense of unity you must have known that you had it before you lost it. Otherwise you couldn't know what you'd lost.

A person doesn't know this in the normal way, which is a recognition of something consciously by the mind. There is simply a sense of something missing, something I've lost in becoming an individual and becoming separate. We could talk about where that sense resides but it doesn't really matter. The suggestion here is that this sense is what gives rise to the subsequent stories that follow. Whatever stories then arise are really about the illusion that 'I', a separate individual, can find whatever it is that I have lost. These stories might be about finding it through religion or through spiritual development or through getting lots of power or through wealth or through relationship or through finding out what my dharma is, what my proper reason is for being on the planet. The stories will tend to revolve around meaning in some way.

What is it that brings about the change which enables us to see all of this as a story?

I think 'change' is an inaccurate word but nevertheless there is the suggestion here that this sense of being a separate individual who is always dissatisfied can fall away. What produces this change, if you want to call it a change, is nothing. It is simply an uncaused spontaneous happening.

When we ask "What brings about this change", we're asking a very obvious question about cause and effect. But cause and effect have no bearing here. This is one of the points that the mind bangs its head against, the statement that cause and effect do not apply. In fact this can't be seen by a person. It can only be seen when the person drops away. Then it's suddenly seen that there never was any possibility that anything that the person apparently did could have caused that dropping away, because the person never did anything. This is why, out of the many possible reactions to a moment of awakening, two of the common ones are laughter or despair.

Both of these can easily be accounted for. Laughter can arise when it's suddenly seen that for the whole of the previous forty or fifty or sixty years there never was anyone who could have done anything to purify themselves so that they could get rid of themself. It can be seen as such an incredible joke that there ever was a sense that 'I' was doing anything.

Or there might be the equally obvious reaction of despair. There might have been many years of doing things to make myself, an inadequate person, become more adequate. Then suddenly it's seen that none of that has any bearing at all, yet the sense of inadequacy may still be there. Seeing this can produce despair. After awakening there may be a desert. It's as if we've suddenly outgrown all the toys in the nursery but there aren't any new toys to replace them. We're surrounded by jack-in-the-boxes when what we want is an electric train. We've grown bored with the jack-in-the-boxes but no one's brought us an electric train. What's more, we can't see how we can possibly get one.

Where are you with this and where have you been with it in the past?

The possibly infuriating answer is that I'm not anywhere and I haven't been anywhere in the past. That's all part of a story which makes sense to a person, but when the person drops away it makes no sense at all. It's seen that there never was a person, there isn't a person now and there isn't any time in which a person could ever have done anything.

Why do you say that's a possibly infuriating answer?

There are many possible reactions to hearing this, a variety of mental and emotional reactions. One of them may be that it's infuriating. It can provoke a lot of anger. It used to provoke some anger here.

When the person disappears, is it the ego that drops away?

'Ego' is a difficult word because it can mean different things to different people. What I'm talking about here is the complete dropping away of the sense of there being a person. It's seen that there is no person whatsoever, there is simply empty awareness in which phenomena arise. That's not what most people mean when they use the phrase 'dropping the ego.' What is usually meant psychologically by the ego might be a part of what drops away, but what I'm trying to describe is the loss of something beyond the ego. The ego might for example become more translucent in various circumstances such as during peak experiences, or through the practice of various spiritual techniques. In these ways the ego can become thinner, as it were, but not drop away entirely. But that has got nothing to do with the dropping away of the person. The person is not the ego.

You have had experience of meditation. Would you say that it's a good thing to practise?

Firstly, there is no one meditating and no choice about meditating so in a sense the question could be seen as irrelevant. Meditation will take place or it won't and there's no one who can do anything about that. But in the story, if there's a person who feels dissatisfied and separate and who feels that they can choose to do something about this, I would say that meditation is a wonderful thing to do.

A metaphor used to express this is of a person who feels that they can make their prison more comfortable. Meditation can't get us out of our prison, but as long as we're in prison, if there's an impulse to do meditation it is one of the things which is most likely to make our prison more comfortable. Meditation is more likely to make our prison comfortable than alcoholism, for example. Ultimately, being a meditator has no more and no less to do with non-duality than being an alcoholic, but being an alcoholic tends to make the prison quite uncomfortable.

Psychotherapy is also likely to make the prison more comfortable. And sometimes I feel like adding shopping. *(Laughter)*

It depends on the character.

You say that meditation is better than alcoholism. Didn't Guru Raj do both?

(Laughing) I don't think I can be held accountable for Guru Raj's practices.

Who's Guru Raj?

There's a story in my first book about Guru Raj. He was a real figure. However unlikely the story sounds, it is true.

I followed Guru Raj for a while. I thought he was a talented teacher and very insightful.

Oh yes, he was. But the whisky and the women weren't exactly what he was teaching.

So that was a true story?

It was a true story. When we feel that we are people looking for salvation, some of us search out someone who is charismatic and who seems to be able to give us amazing experiences. There are hundreds of teachers who can do that. It's a wonderful symbiotic relationship, a wonderful collusion. I, a seeker, offer my devotion to you. You, a guru, offer your charisma to me. Guru Raj taught some extremely powerful meditation techniques and there were some great experiences. For a person who is so inclined, it is impossible not to see the practice of those spiritual techniques as getting 'me' somewhere closer to personal liberation or enlightenment. It's part of the story and it can be a delightful story.

And it's a good way to make a living?

Well, we've all got to make a living. And it cannot be seen through until the person who thinks it's getting them somewhere isn't there anymore. Or rather, it can be seen through in one sense. It can be seen through in the sense that it was in the story of Guru Raj. There was a great explosion of scandal and gossip and most of his teachers left his organisation. But that's not a real seeing through, because what happens then is that everybody thinks "Oh my God, he's not worthy of my devotion ..."

Disillusion?

Yes, disillusion. Then we might go off to find someone else who is worthy of our devotion. It's not a seeing through the appearance, it's just a seeing through that particular individual or character. Nevertheless, for the person that can be a great inoculation against going to other gurus. But then what's going to happen? The person is either going to find another way of seeking or they may fall into despair. Those are the two most likely things to happen.

So what was Guru Raj offering people?

He was very charismatic. He had very powerful meditation techniques. And there are many other gurus and teachers out there who you could say the same thing about. There are many techniques which apparently offer you spiritual growth on the way to an ultimate goal known as personal enlightenment and one of the things to understand about them is that in the story, many of these techniques do produce very real phenomena. Just as taking drugs produces real phenomena. This is why they can be so powerful and so attractive. It's not self-delusion, it's not a case of "I am fooling myself."

Is it like someone feeding you when you're feeling hungry?

You could say there's a parallel. But of course when we eat we just expect our hunger to go away. We're not expecting that to move us towards personal enlightenment. Whereas when we give our devotion to someone like Guru Raj, we're expecting it to get us nearer to a desirable spiritual goal.

But if there's actually no such thing as reality, they're both equally illusory.

Or equally real. When we talk about things being illusory we need to be quite careful. We could say they are equally real or equally unreal. There's no suggestion here that there's anything wrong with giving our devotion or our heart to a 'false guru' (I'm using that phrase rather provocatively perhaps). I'm not suggesting that this is inferior or superior to becoming an alcoholic, going racing or going to meetings about non-duality, because there's no meaning to any of it. There's no choice and of course it's worse than that, there's no one who can make a choice.

It seems to be impossible to hold on to the idea that I don't have any choice, that I didn't have a choice about coming here today. It seems to be impossible to see through that.

It is impossible for a person to see through that. 'You', the unreal person who seems to be making those choices, cannot see the reality that 'you' are unreal. Nevertheless that sense of being a person can fall away. And then it is as incontrovertible that there was no one who ever made a choice as it seems to a person that there is someone who often makes a choice. It becomes just as obvious when the person drops away that this isn't the case as it's been for the previous fifty years that this was the case.

It's a curious thing that if I look at past choices then very often I can see that actually I couldn't have done anything else.

Yes but that's a different thing. We can demonstrate logically to you that really you had no choice about anything. We can get you to analyse all the conditions that happened prior to any choice, including your genes, your parentage and your cultural conditioning. In a sense that's irrelevant. It's not what I'm talking about because that's to do with proving something to the mind through a logical demonstration. And the mind can argue anything, including proving that I personally didn't have any choice because of my genetic structure and the influence of my parents and so on. But so what? Now we have a person who believes that they didn't have any choice instead of a person who thought that they did. But we still have a person. When the person drops away it's simply seen that there never was a person to make a choice. What's more, there never was any time in which any choices could have been made.

What is it that makes it so powerfully obvious to me that there is a person, a person who keeps on going year after year?

Nothing. Out of nothing arise all phenomena, and one of the phenomena that arises most powerfully is the sense that all the other phenomena are experienced by a person. Another way of saying this is it's a mystery. We can make up all sorts of stories about what this mystery consists of. Some of these stories can be very convincing, particularly if we are drawn to the scientific ones. But ultimately it simply happens. Out of nothing arise phenomena, including the phenomenon that I'm a person. This can't be seen through until it drops away, because there's no one to see through it.

There are also some very convincing stories about the mind, about how the mind works and about the levels of the mind. But when this is seen it's like a knife cutting through all of these stories because it's suddenly realised that there is no such thing as a mind. There is simply a thought and then in the story of time another thought. However, they come so thick and fast and they have so much energy that they create the impression that there is something solid behind them called a mind.

There's nothing thinking thoughts. We could also say that there's Nothing thinking thoughts. The mind is an illusion created by the energy of thought. When the person drops away this becomes obvious. The idea that the mind could ever achieve anything becomes ridiculous because the mind is just a thought and a thought can't do anything. It can't analyse another thought. One of the things that this throws light on is the practice of a person trying to calm down their mind by controlling their thoughts. Thought can't stop itself. The previous thought can't stop the next one coming.

But don't thoughts cause actions?

Apparently. But what I'm suggesting is that phenomena simply arise and amongst those phenomena are thoughts. The thought might arise "I'm going to make myself a cup of coffee" and then an action might arise and the body moves across the room towards the kitchen.

So isn't there a person with a body and a mind who can think one thought or a different thought and cause one action or a different action to happen?

A person doesn't have a body or a mind because there is no such thing as a person. There is a psycho-physical organism; phenomena arise; amongst these phenomena are thoughts; these thoughts are likely to give rise to the impression that there's a mind; that's very likely to create the sensation of someone making a choice and causing an action to happen. But all of this is just a story which falls away when it's seen that there's no person who could ever have a thought or ever cause an action. Then it's seen that thoughts simply arise and fall away and so do actions.

What about labelling? Does labelling things cause the person to feel real? Does the way they label things make a difference to their reality?

When you say 'labelling', do you mean using words?

Yes, using words, naming things.

It may make a difference in the story of a person. If this psycho-physical organism is born as an Inuit, by the age of ten there may be several different ways of labelling snow. The perception of snow and the labels used about it may be very different if I am born in Surrey. You could say that the phenomena that arise for the Inuit are going to be different to the phenomena that arise for the child in Surrey and the language is also going to be different. That's just a natural part of the story.

People have different perceptions. The phenomena that arise for this person are different to the phenomena that arise for that person. It's quite clear that language structures experience to some extent and experience structures language. But in the end there are just phenomena.

But whatever the difference in the experience of individuals, we all have the feeling of being a person.

To call it a feeling can be misleading. I recognise a feeling. If I'm sad, or if there's a physical sensation such as hot or cold, that is recognised. But being a person isn't necessarily recognised as such because it's so much an unchanging part of everything that I've ever experienced about life and about the world. Because it arises as soon as there is self-consciousness, it is all 'I' as an individual have known. It has always been there and because of that it's not recognised until it falls away. Then I might say "My God! It never was like that at all."

Somebody suggested during the tea break that the reason for saying that there's absolutely nothing we can do, the reason for this apparent pessimism, is because in a way it gets the mind out of the way. Is there a truth in that?

There's too much cause and effect there so I'd be suspicious of that. I'm not saying "There's nothing you can do." I'm saying "There is no one." That's quite different. And I wouldn't ascribe any reason to anything I say. It's just what's happening. What you said sounds too purposeful.

But the reason for saying this is it gets the possibility of the mind grasping onto something out of the way.

There's no mind to be got out of the way. Thoughts simply arise. As long as there's a person, thoughts of seeking will arise. These thoughts could be about any form of seeking. They could be about seeking for a new party dress. But for somebody who goes to talks on non-duality, they are more likely to be about spiritual seeking.

Nothing that I say or anyone says can possibly stop seeking arising if that's what is happening. For the seeker there may be many different reactions to hearing this, but among the most common are relief, despair, frustration or irritation. These are four quite common responses to hearing this communication.

Or anger?

If the seeker is a bit more psychologically evolved they'll feel anger rather than irritation. Or rage if they're even more evolved. *(Laughter)*

Ascribing purpose is something a person does. There is no purpose.

There is no purpose to the dream?

There is no purpose to the dream. We haven't got particularly philosophical this afternoon. Sometimes there's an impulse, depending on the interests of the characters who have gathered, for a meeting like this to get quite philosophical. I enjoy that, but I also have a resistance to it because what is being offered here is just a description. It's not a philosophy or a set of opinions. It's simply a description of what is seen when the person drops away. That's all.

You're not actually telling us how to do that?

No. Would you like me to? *(Laughter)*

You're damned right I would!

I can tell you lots of things you could do and charge you a huge amount of money. If you like, I'll run workshops. But I feel inclined to say that if I ever write a practical workbook or a group-leaders handbook on how to become liberated, then please put me in a nursing home for the terminally deluded. *(Laughter)*

I'll help you to do the marketing for all of that.

I'd like one of those inspiring little year books, 365 pages, each with an elevating non-duality quote on it.

How about an advent calendar?

When you open up the doors, they'll just be blank. That will be terrible. We'll have children weeping their hearts out all over the country.

I think the doors should be unopenable. (Laughter)

Even better.

****

Can you speak about how it happened? It sounds a bit like Saint Paul's experience on the road to Damascus.

Does it? Oh bugger.

Do you think there's a similarity? It changed him and he wanted to communicate that to other people.

Is the question about an experience or is it about someone wanting to convert people?

I'm only asking because he said it happened in a flash. And equally it sounded indescribable. He suddenly saw everything more brightly.

It's important to remember that awakening is not the final dropping away of the person. The person comes back and the way they've been cultured is likely to colour their interpretation of the event that's just happened.

If they have been cultured to believe that a flash of insight from God may come, then that's quite likely to be the way they will interpret it when they come back. For example, what Hildegard of Bingham says is couched in the language of Christian mysticism because that is her culture. So your question is impossible to answer. After awakening the person comes back and may lay claim to the event that happened, even when it has been seen clearly that there is nobody. When they come back they may ignore this and go "Gee! That was something I achieved by my thirty years of spiritual practice, or because I have been chosen by God so that I can go out and convert others." Or they may tell any one of hundreds of other stories about the event.

I was at a talk recently given by two representatives of Soka Gakkai International. This is a bizarre Japanese Buddhist sect, so bizarre that it's not usually recognised as Buddhist by other Buddhists. Their practice is to chant. It's a lovely chant to listen to. They face a mandala on an altar and they chant to it to bring about whatever they desire. It might be world peace, enlightenment and a Mercedes Benz. As far as they're concerned, this is the complete and absolute answer to everything.

There are hundreds of these stories. And there are hundreds of practices and many of them tend to produce real phenomena. We were talking before about Guru Raj. His practices produced astonishing phenomena. But that has nothing to do with liberation.

If these practices didn't produce phenomena they wouldn't be so seductive. In using the word 'seductive' I'm not implying that there's anything wrong with them. Of course there isn't. I very much enjoyed following my whisky guru for a few years. It was delightful.

****

There often seems to be a gap between awakening and liberation.

In the story of time that seems to happen.

I was wondering whether that's because for the person it would be too powerful energetically for it to happen any other way.

Awakening and liberation are both energetic shifts and they can be extremely powerful. They have nothing to do with under-standing or knowledge or with the apparent mind. There are a few accounts where that energetic shift has produced rather cata-strophic psychological and emotional responses in the person.

Awakening is the sense of contraction opening for a second? Lib-eration is the sense of contraction opening permanently?

You could put it in those terms. In awakening the sense of being a person can fall away, to return half a second later.

Contraction may not be experienced as such by the person, because they've never known any other state since they became self-conscious. They may not feel themselves to be contracted although they might feel uncomfortable in all sorts of emotional and psychological ways. But if there's never been a sense of expan-sion, there can't be anything to feel contracted from.

I get a sense of contraction. It's very uncomfortable.

Sometimes it can be particularly felt after awakening. It can be very distressing then. It can be like a desert because after awak-ening there's been a taste of expansion but now it's gone.

111

Can it be scary? It sounds as if we could feel completely isolated, with no one around to understand.

It can be scary if you read some accounts. But it wasn't for me. Here there was more of a sense of 'Wow' followed by a feeling of disappointment at being a person again. And after that, there was a misinterpretation of what had happened, because the mind was back. The misinterpretation was in thinking that this instant of seeing was complete and that I could regain it and make it permanent. There was no way that I could see that it was actually incomplete. So I misinterpreted it in that sense. I did have quite an active mind and I spun many fine stories about what might happen next.

I would imagine that liberation must be terrifying.

There's no 'must be' about it. It could be. It might have helped that I'd been going to see Tony Parsons regularly before this, but I get the sense that what was seen here wouldn't have been terrifying in any case. Maybe without going to see Tony I might still have gone "Wow", rather than feeling fear. There was nothing about it that I sense would have sent me into fear. It's a very individual thing. If you read Suzanne Segal's account, it sent her into terror.

I'm reading her book and she was very frightened.

From her own description of what happened for her, terror clearly arose for a long time and very powerfully. But that doesn't seem to be common.

Awakening or liberation could have you locked up in a psychiatric ward.

I think that someone who reports that there's no one here but without any expression of distress or discomfort is not likely to end up in psychiatric care. But if there's a lot of distress being expressed as well, then possibly they could.

I've heard about someone who saw this and he started talking about it to his family. He wanted to put his family right. They thought he should see a psychiatrist but fortunately someone suggested that he talk to someone who knew about this first. It was just luck. Otherwise he'd have been sent off to a psychiatrist.

The important phrase there was that "he wanted to put his family right." That's a very tactless thing to do. Anyone who wants to put their family right might be shoved off to see a psychiatrist. *(Laughter)*

But you can imagine liberation happening to someone and they want to get people around them to see "It's not like that." I'm not saying he did it in a self-righteous way. I'm just saying that he started to explain to them what was going on for him. And they tried to send him to see a psychiatrist.

It can happen. It might depend on what stories the people around you follow. If they follow a fundamentalist religious belief for example and you start talking about this, who knows what they might suggest that involves psychiatrists. Or they might want to involve priests, witch doctors or exorcists.

You can see how it might happen. If the character expresses a lot of fear the people around them might get very worried. It's so different from their normal comprehension.

From Suzanne Segal's description, in her case there was a very powerful awakening. Then fear arose and went on arising. In those circumstances it's quite sensible to seek out psychotherapeutic help.

The problem was that she listened to people around her. People around her told her there was something wrong.

She does express a great deal of distress. There was no question of her simply saying to people around her "Look, there's no one here" and them saying "Gosh, you'd better see a psychiatrist." From her own account she was obviously in an extremely painful emotional place, a place of fear about what was happening. I wouldn't criticise the psychotherapists involved. They were responding to her distress rather than to her saying she wasn't there. They were responding to her emotional distress in a way that made sense to them.

There was such a huge shift of energy for her. It completely fragmented her way of being. But there's still an expectation from a lot of people that if this happens then life will become wonderful.

That's the seductive story of personal enlightenment.

But life is just what it is. It's full of stuff and we just call it good stuff or bad stuff.

Yes, it's just what's happening. It's just phenomena arising. But one of the most seductive ideas for a person who becomes fascinated by the thought of spiritual awakening is that it will bring about personal peace and perhaps unending bliss. It's one of the most fascinating ideas about enlightenment. But it's no more seductive than the idea that if I allow the lamb of God into my heart I'll be saved and go to heaven or that if I die as a martyr I'll get seventy two virgins in the after life. Or if the other translation's right, seventy-two crystal clear currants.

I'd rather have the virgins. (Laughter)

Yes, but you don't get a choice. There is a theory that the phrase has been mistranslated so a martyr actually gets seventy-two crystal clear currants.

That's quite a difference. Seventy-two virgins or a small pile of currants.

It is a bit of a difference.

We should spread this news around.

That's what the author who wrote about this theory suggested. He felt it might be a better world if would-be martyrs thought they were going to get a little bowl of currants.

Perhaps they wouldn't be quite so enthusiastic.

But it is no more and no less of a delusion to think that somehow I can obtain personal enlightenment. That's just bliss while the body's still alive, rather than bliss in an after life where I'll be able to laugh at all of you rotting in hell because you are followers of non-duality. It's the same sort of delusion. The core of all these delusions is the belief that somehow there is personal continuation, that I am a person who can continue, whether in heaven or in a state of enlightenment.

****

Are the experiences that come from practising spiritual techniques anything to do with this? It seems that in meditation, the sense of a person somehow gets thinner.

I practised spiritual techniques for many years and there were many experiences which I might describe similarly as a thinning of the person, sometimes to such an extent that the person almost felt translucent. I fully believed that these experiences were moving me towards something called personal enlightenment or personal liberation. It was impossible not to believe that because the evidence seemed to be clearly there.

In awakening this was seen through. Even though 'I' came back, there was no possibility any more of seeing this thinning of the person as anything other than another personal experience. Even in the most transcendental state 'I' was still there having the experience, no matter how translucent 'I' had become.

I can recall standing outside my door about to go to work and

115

experiencing everything as happening right now, literally as if the buildings had just sprung up like mushrooms. It was as if the street was brand new.

There is sometimes a period during which this may be seen as absolutely extraordinary. "Mountains are no longer mountains."

The words "This is the first morning of the world" came into my mind. It was as if 'it' had just come into being in front of my eyes.

It had. That's exactly what had happened. Or rather that's exactly what is happening 'right now'.

7

Nobody Feels Grown Up

Once the sense of separation arises, once self-consciousness arises, the mind starts creating wonderful stories around what all this apparent drama must be about. The sense of separation brings the sense that there's a past, there's a future and there's a journey from the first to the second travelling through the present moment. It's felt that this journey is probably meaningful and we can somehow find out what this meaning is. For some people the meaning might be very simple. It might be hedonistic, revolving around how we can organise our life so we can have more pleasure. But for many of us it's a great deal more complicated and we're not satisfied unless we create stories of the utmost complexity full of religious meaning, spiritual meaning or philosophical meaning to sustain us.

There's a good reason why sometimes these stories have to become immensely complex. If we strip their many complications away, they often become rather easy to see through and therefore no longer satisfying to the mind. If we look at them completely baldly they can have a tendency to dissolve into dust.

So one of the functions of the mind is to evolve ever-increasing complexity so it can remain satisfied with its own stories. The more complex the story becomes, the more convincing it is. The minds thinks "Surely a story about which so many books have been written, about which so many great buildings of stone have been built where important-looking men rush about doing urgent work, surely that story must have some foundation in truth." Often, if the mind starts to doubt its stories, instead of abandoning them it will evolve another layer of complexity, obfuscation and mystification.

The Catholic Church has just abolished Limbo. Before doing this, the Pope set up a commission of theologians to decide whether Limbo still existed. A commission of theologians deciding whether Limbo exists appears very impressive in terms of establishing support for your story. But it's still about a fantasy.

We start off with a simple thought. Then it becomes an idea, then a belief, then a faith, then we have buildings and before we know it there's a commission of theologians looking into whether Limbo exists. If that's the fantasy we're entranced by, it can seem both convincing and important. It's an example of how desperate for story and meaning we can be.

For a person who feels a sense of separation, wandering around the park looking at the trees often doesn't seem to be enough. There seems to be something missing and so we start to make up all the stories to give our lives purpose.

We're sharing this building today with a Jungian association. This started me thinking about the different psychological stories we tell. Psychological stories try to make sense of the inner mess which we might feel ourselves to be in, rather than looking for outward salvation. Most of the psychological stories can be divided into two kinds, can be placed in one of two baskets. At the bottom of each of these two baskets is a particular concept of what a human being is at their core.

One of the baskets contains the concept that at our centre we are a mass of contradictory impulses. This is generally held in some form by the psychologies that have developed directly from Freud. In stories like these, the purpose of therapy is to bring about some kind of resolution between these contradictory impulses so that we can live in relative peace. The hope is that these conflicts and contradictions can somehow be resolved or harmonised so that they can live together without being at war.

At the bottom of the other basket is the concept that at our centre there is what could be called our authentic self, our real self, or our core self. These psychologies, usually known as Humanistic, hold that if we can only contact our real self, if we can clear out everything that gets in the way of that, then we will know what we really want out of life and our life may then flow because our energies will be directed towards this coherent aim. Only then will we feel fulfilled in our relationships, our work, and our life. Transpersonal psychologies add to this the notion that, at its deepest level, the nature of our core self is spiritual.

These are two very different beliefs about what lies at the heart of an individual. On the one hand we're a mass of contradictory impulses which need to be resolved, on the other hand we have an authentic self which is waiting to be discovered. Those of us who have some knowledge of Indian philosophy might readily relate the idea of an authentic self to the idea of dharma and we won't be surprised to learn that the 'core self' psychologies have been influenced by Eastern philosophies. Put simply, the theory of dharma is that there is a purpose and a meaning to our life which is important to our spiritual evolution. We need to discover what our dharma is and if we then align ourself with it and follow it, our life will be fruitful and possibly harmonious.

So the two baskets of psychologies are very different but they each tell a coherent story about what a human being consists of. Freudian psychologists and Humanistic or Transpersonal psychologists are able to tell us a logical and convincing story which holds together very well.

However, in liberation there is a falling away of the sense of being an autonomous individual who makes meaningful choices about a journey through time called 'my life'. Then what lies at the centre of an individual is seen very clearly. It is nothing or No Thing. It is emptiness. Out of that emptiness come all these stories, that we are a mass of contradictions which we need to

119

resolve or that we have an authentic self or a spiritual self that we need to discover. Out of emptiness the sense of a separate person arises, bringing with it the many stories about what we are.

It can be a great shock when the sense of being a separate person falls away, because these stories about our nature are suddenly seen through. Then it's seen that we are emptiness. Before we fall into existential despair about this, let me suggest that we are also fullness.

Would you also call this a story or would you consider it to be a mystery? Or is it just another story to say that I don't really know what's going on anymore?

Everything that can be put into words or thoughts is a story. I am telling a story here, but it's the story which describes what is as closely as possible. Other stories tend to add unnecessary complexity to this. So understanding that "I don't know what's going on anymore" is also a story. It has to be. There's nothing else it can be.

But acknowledging that this is a mystery, that it cannot be known through the mind, is close to what is. Thinking that I understand it and that I know what I have to do to get into heaven, or to come back in a new incarnation as a more enlightened soul, is a long way away from what is.

We could say that being in a state of not-knowing is closer to a description of this, because this is a mystery. But I don't want to imply a method here. I don't want to suggest that we should give up thinking that we know the meaning of life and be in a state of not-knowing. This will do us no good because there is no one who can do it.

Whether we see a mass of contradictions or an authentic self at our centre, it's equally a story. But if it is seen that there is only emptiness at our centre, it is realised that this is a mystery and life is lived in not-knowing. Everything is arising spontaneously from nothing. That is the ultimate mystery.

Could we explain the mystery by saying that God made it?

God didn't make it. But this manifestation seems so solid that it doesn't seem to make any sense for someone to sit here and say "This is empty." Yet in the story of history, this has been seen over and over again in many different cultures. It doesn't have anything particularly to do with Advaita. It is sometimes talked about and it is nearly always misunderstood.

There was a Christian mystic, Marguerite Porete, who lived at the end of the thirteenth century and was executed as a heretic at the beginning of the fourteenth century. Surprisingly some of her writing survived. She writes about seeing Nothing, about immersion in the Abyss, about an identity with the divine in a nothingness which is at the same time the All. "Now this soul has fallen from love into nothingness, and without such nothingness she cannot be All."

Although Marguerite Porete belonged to a lay religious order, she had little time for virtue. She wrote of the virtuous as 'sad ones' leading a sad life and she felt that virtue led to a sterile, arid place. She wrote that the pursuit of virtue could be useful for some people, but only because it might lead them into a lifeless desert where they might give up in despair. Then another possibility could arise.

There doesn't seem to have been much reference to liberation in Christianity.

For centuries in Western culture, if people communicated about seeing this, they ran the risk of being executed and their writings being burnt. It's surprising that even a few references to this have survived. There were probably others who saw this but who kept quiet. If I had lived in medieval Europe under the Inquisition, I wouldn't have talked about this. I would have been in my allotment quietly hoeing and chanting from my prayer book.

I gave a talk recently where somebody referred to this as a new message. It's not a new message. It's been seen at different times in different places by different people. We have no idea how many people have seen it. It was very dangerous to talk about it for long periods of history. There are many places where it would be very dangerous to talk about it today. I don't think we'd be holding these talks if we were in Kabul right now.

Meister Eckhart also saw this. He cheated the Inquisition. He escaped execution for heresy by the simple trick of dying before his trial ended. He writes about real poverty having nothing to do with destituting ourselves or divesting ourselves of possessions. Poverty, he says, is having nothing because there is no one.

This overthrows all authority.

This is a recurring message. It keeps being seen. It can't be killed off. The Church can't kill it off. The Taliban can't kill it off. Evolutionary spiritual paths, which entrance us by promising that there is something we can do to bring ourselves nearer to enlightenment, can't kill it off either. It requires nothing. It requires no churches, no philosophical tracts, no scriptures, no history. If everything that had ever been thought, said or written about non-duality were to disappear in a moment, it would simply re-emerge. It would re-emerge because nothing has to be learnt, nothing has to be studied, nothing has to be done, no spiritual purification and no pleasing of God has to take place, for the seeing of liberation to occur. It arises spontaneously. One moment there's somebody there, the next moment there isn't. One moment there's somebody crossing a field, the next moment there's just crossing a field.

Are you saying that when this is seen clearly, Freud's theories, for example, are seen to be unreal, as just stories?

They're real stories which give the individual what they are often desperate for – something that seems to make sense of this. All psychological stories serve the same purpose, even when they seem to be diametrically opposed. The Freudian story and the Transpersonal story can be seen as opposites in a way, yet both fulfil the same purpose, just as all other stories do, including "I will know happiness when I have found the perfect Versace dressing gown." Their purpose is to either make sense of the mess inside me, the psychological mess, or the mess outside me, the mess of the world.

Some psychologists and therapists acknowledge the 'story nature' of their theories. They warn against 'reification', the turning of an idea such as 'the subconscious' or 'sub-personalities' into a thing as if it really existed in any form other than as an idea.

Why do these stories get so complicated?

The more complicated they are, the more effective they are, because then they are more difficult to see through. The story that "I will be happy when I've found the perfect Versace dressing gown" is not a very good one because it's too easy to see through. The Freudian story or the Tibetan Buddhist story are much better because they are wonderfully complex. The Catholic story is beautifully complicated. The committee of theologians discussing Limbo for a year is just one tiny part of it.

The more complex the story, the more real it seems and therefore the more satisfying and comforting it is to the separated, vulnerable individual. It seems particularly real if it is reinforced with buildings, if the story is complex enough for some stones to be erected around it. I mean that literally. The stones might be St Peter's Basilica in Rome or The Psychoanalytic Institute in London. There is something very comforting about having the story we believe in reinforced with buildings, especially if they seem old. It is very difficult to argue with stones.

Do you believe in Freud's view of us?

No. It's a story. It's a real story, which is there to make sense of the mess which we perceive inside us. Other stories are there to make sense of the mess which we perceive outside us. If a story has bricks and mortar or stones around it, it is more convincing. We're in trouble with non-duality because there are no solid buildings. There's no Temple of Non-Duality yet. But there might be one day.

If you go to The College of Psychic Studies in South Kensington, you may be more likely to believe that your dead Uncle is trying to contact you from beyond the grave. It's a very impressive building with a grand wood-panelled meeting room. Who could argue with that?

A lot of stories have a heaviness about them. It's as if the actual buildings weigh down on us. What's left when they're gone?

The utter simplicity of being is left. There's nothing to do, nothing that needs to be done. There's nowhere to go, no one who can go anywhere. This is it and this is enough. This is seen when the sense of separation drops away. And within this, any story can still arise and may still be enjoyed.

Nobody in this room needs to do anything to be. Is there anybody in this room doing being?

The mind wants to be convinced by ever-increasing complexity, sophistication and argument. But no mental constructs that arise have anything to do with seeing this, although some of them are very interesting. There's nothing wrong with mental constructs but they can't touch the absolute simplicity of being. Out of nothing arises the appearance of everything. It's a mystery and then the mind gets to work on it and thinks that it can explain it.

Forget about understanding. Everything that the mind thinks that it understands about this mystery is inadequate.

The stories get very complex, don't they?

As long as there is the sense that there is a mind functioning as an entity, that mind will probably like complexity. It doesn't have to be philosophical complexity of course. It could be a complex way of working out which horse is going to win the Cheltenham Gold Cup.

What about when the complex stories fall away? Are you left with simplicity?

When the stories are seen through, what is seen is absolute simplicity. You can't have more simplicity than nothing, the abyss from which everything arises including all the complexities.

It's only the mind that makes everything seem so complex.

Yes, but until the mind is seen through, that can't be seen. Being expresses itself as wonderfully complex theories about the meaning of life. When they are seen through, they are seen to be empty. They might still be fascinating but they won't be taken seriously.

It sounds as if this woman who you quoted, Marguerite, is just describing concepts.

It sounds like that because she's using words to describe the indescribable. What she says is about as close as you can get to this in words. There is nothing. There is the abyss. 'Abyss' doesn't sound very comforting, does it? But it is only when that is seen that it can be realised that 'I' am the all. When it is seen that I am nothing, it can be seen that I am everything.

It sounds like an experience.

It may sound like that, but she is attempting a description of what is seen when there is no one there to have an experience.

She sounds like she's describing a vision.

But she isn't. It's so difficult to get close to this in language. If I had a magic wand, I could wave it and instead of a person sitting there listening to a talk there would just be sitting there listening to a talk. Then what we are trying to describe here would be clear.

The fact that she's making a distinction between nothing and the abyss tells me that to some extent she's conceptualising.

There's no distinction at all. Nor is there a distinction when I say that the abyss is a full abyss. I'm just doing what I can with language to express the paradoxical nature of the seeing of this, the seeing that there is emptiness but that it is a full emptiness.

That might not be very helpful but it's the best I can do.

I don't understand this description of a full empiness.

If you ask me how emptiness can be full, I can't answer that question, I can only report that it is. If you ask me what it's full of, all I can say is love. This is why it's possible to say that there is only love. But there's not much that the mind can do with that. The mind is likely to start arguing against it. If you look at the world of phenomena, there's a lot of basis to argue against it, there's a lot that doesn't look like love. I could argue against it myself. When you let the mind have its say, it will win. Put nothing and the mind up against each other in an argument and the mind will win. Ultimately, emptiness full of love is either seen or it's not seen.

How can I bypass the mind?

You can't bypass the mind because you're trying to bypass something which does not exist. The mind is a process of thought in a story of time. Thoughts arise out of nothing and there is no one, so who is going to bypass thoughts?

But the desire to bypass them does occur.

That's another thought. The thought that I would like to bypass my thoughts certainly contains some contradictions.

Does the mind actually exist? Does self-consciousness exist?

The mind only exists as thoughts. Self-consciousness arises as a thought, or a sense, that there is a separate entity here who is doing the thinking. It's a particularly addictive and repetitive thought. "I exist" is the most repetitive thought there is.

It's part of the story?

It's part of the story. Out of nothing arises the thought that there is an autonomous individual here. But as that is just a thought, there is no one who can get rid of it. As long as there is an out-pouring from nothing of the sense that there is an individual here, that's going to seem to be the case. As there is nobody here, there's no one who can destroy that sense or who can meditate themselves out of it or who can go to a guru and receive a trans-mission of energy that will make their self disappear. That which is trying to get itself to disappear doesn't exist. It's simply a dis-embodied thought, although I know it doesn't seem disembodied to a person. An analogy that's often used traditionally is that the pot can't understand the potter. Of course, it's not a very good analogy because there is no potter. Let's just say that a thought can't understand the Nothing from which it arises.

That's why people are occasionally stunned into a couple of years of silence when this is seen through. Everything I thought, everything I believed, everything I held to be true and real about myself, is seen to mean nothing.

I've heard this seeing described as intimacy with everything.

It's absolute intimacy, because what is seen is that you are both nothing and everything. It's more than intimacy. Intimacy sug-gests duality, two which are connected. Oneness goes beyond intimacy.

Intimacy implies two?

Yes, it's an 'I' 'Thou' word.

What about compassion? How would you describe compassion?

When the person is seen through, it may be realised that it is very difficult to be a person. That can give rise to compassion.

It's tough being a person. It may be so tough for me that I don't notice how tough it is for other people. When the person leaves and the house is empty, there may be space to notice for the first time how tough it is for others. That's related to compassion.

The difficulty of being a person explains much of what goes on in the drama, including a lot of the very unpleasant stuff. Being a person can feel so awful that we sometimes have to do really horrible things in order to make ourselves feel better. Of course this is a story about individuals who can apparently choose whether to do nice things or horrible things.

What about the description you get in the spiritual traditions of Satchitananda? Is that the nature of the absolute?

Yes. There's energy and there's consciousness, otherwise there wouldn't be the appearance of anything. And everything is unconditional love. It just doesn't look like love at times because we're viewing everything through the prism of being an individual. When the pure white light of being hits the prism of individual consciousness, out come the many colours of the rainbow, including a few rather muddy colours that the individual may not like.

Could we translate Satchitananda as 'energy, understanding and bliss'?

I'm a bit suspicious of 'understanding'. It sounds too conceptual. I like 'energy, consciousness, love'. The word 'bliss' can set too many hares running across our mind. "Ooo! There must be a state of constant bliss!" Well, you could try taking heroin.

Everything changes. Everything is impermanent. The idea of a permanent state of any kind for the embodied individual is nonsense. For the psycho-physical organism, everything is in constant flux.

When everything is seen as unconditional love, is it seen inside me?

No. It's seen neither inside myself nor outside myself, because there is no me. It's only seen when the self is not there. Unconditional love is never seen by the person. In liberation, when the person is not there, it is seen that the nature of Nothing is unconditional love.

The phrase 'unconditional love' is not a comforting phrase, it's a fierce phrase. It's impossible for an individual to really conceive of unconditional love, no matter what spiritual philosophy we may embrace. We may have it as a poorly understood concept but it cannot be experienced by an individual.

There is a Buddhist text, almost certainly a fake from many centuries after the Buddha's death, that has the Buddha saying that if you are being tortured slowly to death by your enemies over agonising hours and you allow yourself to have one angry or unforgiving thought about your torturers, then you are not a true follower of his.

This is an invention of the mind – the idea that it is possible for an individual to be in this state of unconditional love where there is utter forgiveness of our torturers as they cut the flesh slowly and agonisingly from our bones. It's ridiculous. For an individual, thoughts arise and they will not all be thoughts of unconditional love – not unless we run the risk of intense mental and emotional constipation. But when the person drops away, none of this matters or is an issue anymore. It is then just seen that unconditional love is the case. You don't have to struggle to see it, you don't have to earn the right to see it, you don't have to be noble like the tortured Buddhist to see it, you don't have to be brave or devoted or spiritually evolved to see it, because it doesn't have anything to do with you. When the person drops away it is simply obvious that unconditional love is the nature of the mystery.

Spiritual stories often become ever more extreme because there are competing sects, each one wanting to prove that they are more pure than the others. There is another Buddhist text, again a fake from long after the Buddha's death, that states that the worst sin we can commit is to persuade a vegetarian to eat meat. This is because by persuading them to eat meat we will be depriving them of their chance of enlightenment. It is thought that this story also developed from competitiveness between Buddhist sects – in this case between a sect that ate meat and a vegetarian sect that wanted to prove that it was more pure.

A spiritual philosophy develops. Very quickly we have sects and the next thing is we are at war with each other. We compete to push the philosophy to extremes, to show that our sect is purer than yours, that we are more virtuous than you. And the more insignificant the distinction between us, the more passionately we will fight to defend it. Freud called this 'the narcissism of small differences'.

****

Why do you say that awakening and liberation are a shock?

Because if we suddenly disappear, every conception that we have of ourself disappears as well. All our beliefs, all our stories, all the ambitions that sustained us, all our achievements, our feeling that because we have meditated for thirty years we may have become a little holier, all of this disappears.

My whole belief system disappeared overnight. Everything I'd taken as real was no longer there. And until that happened, I didn't even know I had those beliefs.

The realisation that there is no individual here can be a tremendous shock. But it can also give rise to a lot of laughter. There can be different reactions to seeing through the story of our life. In my case it was the story of a dedicated spiritual seeker. To see that this has no purpose, no meaning, can be such a joke. All those teachers, all those texts, all those philosophies apparently lasting for thousands of years, drop away in the absolute seeing of this.

****

As I've said before, the Great Mantra is 'Helpless, Hopeless and Meaningless'. Hearing that I am helpless isn't a very comfortable or easy message. As long as there's a person, there will probably be the hope that some help can be found. But looking for help is often very effortful. It's possible that if the person hears that they are helpless, they may recognise that they might as well relax.

Especially if there's a recognition that there isn't really any predicament, even if there is a dislike of their situation?

It's that sense of dislike that's the difficulty. We feel uncomfortable as a person at least some of the time. Therefore there's a predicament and we want to do something about it. Even if there's nothing particularly bad going on and we're not depressed or unhappy, we often feel that this isn't enough. Seeing that this is enough, that it's sufficient in itself, is part of the shock when the person falls away.

Even when there's nothing at all?

As long as there's a body-mind there can't be nothing at all except in dreamless sleep. But what there is can sometimes seem rather dull and lifeless to a person. Remember Plato's famous metaphor of the cave. Plato says that we experience reality as if we are in a cave tied to a chair facing a wall. All we can see are the shadows of the shapes of replicas of real things cast on the wall by the flames of a fire. We're not experiencing reality or even a copy of reality, we're experiencing the shadow of a copy of reality. A modern equivalent would be watching television soaps whilst slumped on a sofa. 'EastEnders' is literally the shadow of a copy of reality.

That's quite empty, quite dull, isn't it? Even when things are going quite well, there is still the predicament that we often don't find them very fulfilling. So we become addicted to things that will temporarily lift our spirits, like shopping or heroin or being blessed by gurus. We'll go to night clubs and snort cocaine or go to gurus and snort shakti but we'll come back to the predicament that this as it is doesn't satisfy us. Even if we understand intellectually and really believe that this is all there is because we've heard that from someone we trust, as a person we often find it unfulfilling.

131

But a simple shopping trip can temporarily lift our spirits. It's no wonder that going to spiritual teachers can lift them. A friend of mine follows a teacher in America who never publicises herself. Her existence is more or less a secret among her followers. If you want to go to see her you have to find your way to her somehow, perhaps through a connection with someone who already knows her. This is already a fascinating story, redolent with meaning. It's a lot more exciting than sitting at home watching television. It may be great for lifting your spirits.

A lot of people feel very good around certain spiritual teachers. Many people feel happy in the presence of their guru. These are simply personal experiences but it's no wonder that we get entranced by them and addicted to them because sitting in a chair, just being, is often not enough for an individual.

I like what Nathan Gill says in 'Clarity' very much. "You may feel the need to become more aware, be here now, enter the stillness ... be blissful ... get rid of the ego ... get enlightened ... While you're busy with all that, I'll go and have a cup of tea and read the paper."

However, as long as there's an individual, it's quite likely that having a cup of tea won't be sufficient.

I used to love shopping. I spent lots of money. Then I lost the urge completely and shopping became functional.

If you like shopping, stay away from non-duality. Flee from it as fast as you can.

I don't need to get a buzz from shopping anymore.

For many of us, it's feeding an addiction. The basic addiction is for something more exciting than this as it's experienced by the person. All the other addictions come from the need to give ourself a lift because this does not seem fascinating enough.

When the person's gone and there isn't separation anymore between the phenomena that arise and the awareness in which they arise, this is no longer seen as dull. Instead it's seen as a miracle.

We don't have to go to Lourdes for a miracle. This is a miracle happening right now.

****

After this is seen, how do you sustain it?

You don't sustain it. You can't sustain anything. It may or may not be sustained.

You can't produce the seeing of this and you can't sustain it. This can't be seen until Nothing is seen. That's what Marguerite Porete is saying. Until we see that we are Nothing, we cannot see that we are All. Until it is seen that all is empty, it cannot be seen that all is full.

When this is seen to be empty of self, it's seen that it's full of love. When self is there and filling this, it blocks out that view.

Nothing has to happen for this to be seen, but you have to understand that sentence in both possible ways.

So it's Nothing that creates all of this?

Yes, the same old boring Nothing pretending to be an exciting something. You could say that it's the existence of the individual self that enables Nothing to pretend that it's something. As long as we're taken in by that pretence, it can't be seen that what's really going on is unconditional love. It can't be seen because we're entranced by the play. The play does not usually look like unconditional love. A lot of it doesn't look like love at all and the bits that do look like love seem to be pretty conditional.

The individual is taken in by the play. The individual takes the play to be real.

I've heard it said, and it's confused me, that in liberation there's a total acceptance of what is, but by no one. That's another way of saying that there's no one there to accept or not accept it anyway. Is there a paradox there? What is acceptance? We can accept that this is a play but that's still not it.

133

There can be an acceptance that this is a play in a variety of ways. One is acceptance of an idea which helps us not to take things too seriously or get too upset about them. So when things go wrong we think "Oh well, it's just a play, it's just a dream. It will all be the same in a hundred years. Dust to dust." We may find that comforting as an idea.

Or a kind of witnessing can arise. This is sometimes referred to as witness consciousness. It has more reality than an intellectual understanding of acceptance. A detachment between our experience and our awareness becomes apparent. Remember that in detachment it is still felt to be our awareness, not awareness itself.

An ability to witness or observe our own experience develops. Here's our individual awareness and there's the experience of the play. There's a standing back from the play, a sense of watching it from a distance. It can seem as if we're standing behind ourself observing life over our shoulder.

That can feel like a very comfortable and strong place. There's a gap between us and experience.

It can feel both comfortable and comforting because it can feel as if experience can't touch us, can't wound us. There is something very attractive about detachment.

It might be a conceptual thing – it might be psychosis.

Psychosis isn't conceptual.
Our awareness and our experience somehow seem separated so awareness is felt to be standing back from experience. This may sometimes be interpreted as psychosis.

It's very difficult to describe it, this gap between awareness and experience.

There's a sense that we're protected from the things that could normally touch us and harm us. Our normal sense of vulnerability is reduced or it isn't there anymore.

Do you think it has a lot to do with control or wanting to control our experience?

There can be an intellectual standing back which involves a sense of control, as if we're trying to force a separation between ourself and the phenomena that we experience. There can also be a sense of detachment which simply arises naturally. There are also certain practices which can give rise to it. There can be a genuine sense of standing back from our experience which isn't forced and isn't controlled.

Just as detachment can be mistaken by some people for psychosis, it can be mistaken by others for enlightenment. But it isn't either of those two things. It's just detachment, a sense of separation between ourself and what we are experiencing. That's very different to the dropping away of the sense that we are an individual. In witness consciousness there is still a form of personal identity, but it seems more subtle than when consciousness is completely caught up in 'our' identity.

I've heard people talk about the field of awareness and that which is known in the field.

That could be a description of detachment or it could be a description of liberation. It's difficult to know from the words. There is awareness and there is the content of awareness, the phenomena that arise. When the individual drops away, the phenomena that were there before still arise. That can sound dualistic, so a better way of putting it would be to say that there is being arising as phenomena. Rather suddenly and shockingly it may be seen that these don't have to include the phenomenon of the self.

When you recognise awareness as your essential nature, then you see awareness as the essential nature of everything. Is that right?

Yes. Except the crucial thing is that *you* don't see that. It is simply seen. There is no 'you' who is experiencing it. 'You' is a redundant idea. But calling it an idea can make it sound rather easy to get rid of 'you' and it isn't. 'You' are neither easy nor difficult to get rid of. 'You' are either there or not there. The idea that it is difficult but possible to get rid of 'you' is what gives rise to many of the evolutionary spiritual paths.

We attach a lot of reality to the self?

For a person it has an intense reality. It can't be got rid of, but it can fall away.

You could say it's a phantom self in a way. But as long as you believe in it, it may as well be real.

It's a phantom self but it seems very real and it's got nothing to do with you believing in it. It's got nothing to do with either you or belief. When there's a sense of an individual, that's not because there's a belief. It's more tangible than that. Changing your beliefs won't get rid of the sense of being an individual.

It's more primary than that?

Yes, it's more primary than a belief. It's a very powerful sensation.

Maybe some people use the word 'God' to mean liberation, this, everything that is.

'God' is what you are, essentially.

But then it gets twisted by religions and God gets turned into a giant super being in the sky. Before it got twisted it must have meant everything that is.

It's our essential nature, which self-consciousness cuts us off from. The dropping away of the self returns us to the state of

136

knowing what we really are. It doesn't matter whether we use the word 'God', 'Consciousness', 'Unity', 'Oneness', 'Awareness', 'Being'. All these words are inadequate. They can only ever be a pointer to something which cannot be seen until it's seen.

Even when it's seen, the mind can come in and argue with it, but its arguments are seen through. In liberation there is a seeing of what we essentially are and in that anything can arise, including the mind saying "Yes, but maybe there is something else. If I went to see another guru perhaps I'd find out what it is." That thought can still arise, but it's seen through, it's seen as another phenomenon. The sound of bird-song arises. A leaf falling from a tree arises. A thought that if I go to see another guru I might discover that there is something more than this arises. These are all just phenomena arising in presence.

It's seen that you're not doing it?

Yes. And it's also seen that in liberation, any phenomenon is still possible. This isn't a comforting message. It's not "Liberation is seen. Great! Bliss, here I come!"

Is it possible that original sin is what splits us off from presence and makes us feel separate?

'Original sin' really refers to the arising of self-consciousness. At a young age a transition is made from 'All is One', but in unconsciousness, to a conscious sense that "I am a separate individual." This might first be felt as the realisation that "I am separate from mummy." Before a certain age there is no recognition that mummy, or anything else, is not part of 'me'.

In the story of the Garden of Eden, we are separated from 'God'. That is, we are separated from our real nature by self-consciousness. The doctrine of 'original sin' wasn't really developed until Saint Augustine in the fifth century. The phrase 'original sin' makes the story of the Garden of Eden much more difficult to interpret. If we ignore this latecomer of a phrase, the story makes much more sense.

Adam and Eve ate the fruit of the tree of knowledge. In other words, they became self-aware. Through becoming self-aware, we lose paradise, or rather we think we do. Suddenly there's separation and personal vulnerability and pain and boredom. So we think "How can this be paradise?" Then we spend the rest of our lives trying to get back into the paradise that we think we've lost.

But all the time that we are trying to get back into paradise, we are already in it because we never left it. Leaving paradise is an illusion created by self-consciousness. The return to paradise can only come about when separation is seen through.

In the first place there was just awareness. What fragmented it or divided it?

At first there is just awareness with no self-consciousness. Then self-consciousness splits us off from the sense that All is One. From then on it seems that there are two things, an aware individual here and everything else out there.

But in a way that original awareness is never really lost?

It's only lost in the appearance, in the story. It's only lost in the cosmic entertainment.

It's not lost in reality?

There is awareness, there is Oneness, there is nothing happening. Oneness never loses itself. It never separates from itself. And in the story, in which time seems to exist, there appears to be a separation into self-consciousness of this little vulnerable individual. From then on awareness seems to belong here and everything else is cut off and out there, including other people. But there will probably be an assumption here that there is awareness in you as well, that you are not robotic. This can only be an assumption because obviously there's no direct knowledge in me of awareness in you. But it seems like a very reasonable assumption. So from now on awareness seems split up into tiny parcels. There's a little aware individual here and there's an assumption that there are lots of other little aware individuals over there.

This is all a story because there is actually nothing happening.

So there's never been a loss?

There's never been a loss because there's nothing happening. But don't expect the individual to make any sense of that. How can an individual make sense of my sitting here and saying "There's nothing happening"? The individual thinks "But I came here today. I left home this morning and I'm hoping to stop off on the way back and have a few drinks before I catch my train."

The very fact that there seems to be a sentence being spoken here with a thought contained in it which has a beginning, a middle and an end surely suggests that there is something happening. So what sense can the individual make of someone sitting here in this chair and a voice saying "Nothing's happening"?

Oneness was never lost. There is only Oneness, but in that a dream of separation apparently takes place.

So all of us who were hoping to catch trains home tonight are in real trouble. There is no tonight, there are no homes and there are no trains to catch.

And no trouble!

No trouble. No problems. No drunken football fans out on the streets.

Is the sense of eternity part of the story?

Eternity is the end of time. Eternity is timeless but in eternity a dream of time arises, in which we were able to come here today on trains, on buses and in cars, and in which we may go to the pub after this talk. The dream can only take place because there is the appearance of time in which events can apparently happen.

Space is also part of the dream of separation. How can there be space when there is only Oneness? Space requires differentiation.

But the self-conscious individual mind has only ever existed in space and time, so it cannot make sense of this.

If we take hallucinogenic drugs, they may distort our sense of space and time so much that there will probably be a realisation that they are at the very least provisional. How we usually experience them is just one possible version of them. Our experience of space and time is created by our particular psycho-physical set-up. If we tinker with this with a small amount of L.S.D., they are likely to be experienced in a radically different way.

It can be quite a shock to realise that space and time are subjective. But this can only be a parallel to what is seen when the person drops away, which is that there is no space and time whatever. They are a fiction, so whether they are provisional or absolute, subjective or objective, makes no difference.

This is why it is asserted here that there is nothing happening. There isn't any time for anything to be happening in.

And nowhere for anything to go?

Yes, nowhere for anything to go.

Language breaks down in trying to describe this. I could say that there is no space because awareness is everywhere, but 'everywhere' implies space so that doesn't work. I could say that everything is interconnected but that's misleading too because it suggests that there are different things. We cannot satisfactorily put this into words.

It might seem that awareness is concretised or individualised here but it isn't. That wall is just as much awareness as the thoughts that seem to arise in this apparent mind.

We think we're seeing things out there but really we're seeing them inside ourselves. We assume there's space between me and you but that's simply an idea. It's all happening in here, in the mind.

All descriptions are metaphorical. They are all trying to reach towards something which can't be explained. Into the prism of the mind comes the white light of undifferentiated being in

140

which there is no space and time. Out of the prism come the many colours of the rainbow, the phenomena which can only exist in space and time.

In emptiness there is no space? Space is part of duality? Really there is no location?

Space is emptiness appearing as location and separateness. Space is part of duality. That's not a philosophical statement. It's an attempt to describe what's seen.

It's a hologram.

That's a good metaphor. It's a particularly clever hologram, a hologram which seems to have solidity.

In a hologram, the whole is contained in all the little bits.

This is just a metaphor. There aren't any little bits.

Discussions about this can become very arcane and abstruse. I remember a discussion at a meeting on non-duality about whether someone had a back to their head or a brain if you couldn't see it. It went on for quite a long time. But what does it matter?

It reminds us that nothing can be known, that nothing is real.

I'll stick to using 'real' to describe whatever phenomena are arising. This glass is real. Beliefs, perceptions, thoughts are real. Whatever is, whatever is appearing, is real. But it's only real in the sense that it is appearing transiently in this. If I have the thought that I will only be saved if I accept the blood of the lamb into my heart, that is a real thought. But it has no reality beyond that. Most 'real phenomena' don't last more than a few seconds.

Sometimes I imagine Oneness must be rolling around on the floor laughing at this big joke called human forms. It's all so absurd.

That's you rolling around on the floor. But it doesn't seem like a joke until the person drops away. Until then, it seems very serious.

Once the person drops away it's no longer serious?

Once the person drops away it can give rise to a lot of laughter. Then the game may be enjoyed as a game. That's what is meant in the New Testament by "Unless you become as little children you cannot enter the kingdom." What do little children do? They enjoy games. They're very good at pretending, at making things up and enjoying it.

I've read that children think that their parents are playing a game as well and that they are shocked when they realise that they really believe what they're doing.

Or they put on a good pretence that they believe it. There was a French priest who said that what he had learnt from a long lifetime of listening to people was that nobody ever felt grown up.

8

Throwing Sticks For Monty

To be a person is to have a sense of volition, a sense of autonomy, a sense that I can make choices and do things of my own accord. For a person there is the sense that I am an individual for whom phenomena arise. This is a very persuasive and addictive sense.

The feeling of being a person is actually itself just another phenomenon which has no more meaning to it than anything else that arises. If the sound of a car is heard, that sound has as much meaning or as little meaning as the sense that it is being heard by an individual who has their own energy which is separate from the energies of other people. The sense that I am a person experiencing phenomena has no more meaning than any one of those phenomena themselves, such as the sound of this voice or the touch of this hand on this arm.

The feeling that I am a person is the central core around which all the other phenomena seem to accrete. They all seem to belong to it. The difference between being asleep and being awake could be summed up in the following way: asleep, there is the sense that there is a separate person for whom everything is happening;

143

awake, this sense of being a separate individual is seen to be just another phenomenon with no other reality.

There is only undifferentiated being arising as apparent difference. Any sense that I have a life and I can make choices falls away when this is seen. This is why we can say that this communication cuts through everything. It cuts through all the stories that we tell about the person. The most gripping stories are the ones about meaning and purpose. We tell ourselves "I have a purpose. My life has meaning." This cuts through all of that because it blows the cover of the individual. It sees that there is no meaning or purpose beyond this itself.

If I seriously asserted to you that this flower in this vase had a purpose and it could become a more fulfilled flower if it took responsibility for itself or if it found God or if it had some floral psychotherapy, you'd probably think I was insane. I'm suggesting to you that to ask questions about my life purpose or about the meaning of my life makes no more sense than to ask these questions about a flower. To use a more traditional metaphor, it makes no more sense than to ask these questions about a wave as if it were a separate entity to the ocean. No matter how much a wave may look like an entity which is separate from the ocean, we know that it is not.

For the onlooker standing on the beach, the waves may appear to give a convincing display of individuality and separateness. Some may look like big important waves with urgent business to accomplish, others may look like humble waves dedicating their life to the service of mankind as they rush towards the shore to meet their destiny. But we know that the waves have no separate existence, that the convincing display is an illusion. They are simply the ocean waving. You are simply the ocean 'personing'.

Watching a play is another good metaphor for this. If the production is convincing, the characters seem like real people with real lives, real pasts and futures and relationships and particularly real choices to be made. For us in the audience, it may be a very convincing display. If we suspend our disbelief and get caught up in the drama, we will see the characters as individuals whose lives are meaningful, who may be good or evil, and who above all have choice. Remove their choice and the whole play falls apart. For example, it seems that Hamlet really does have choice. There he is, caught in his indecision. "Shall I kill the king, or shan't I kill the king? Shall I trust the ghost that says that the king murdered my father, or is the ghost a demon sent to tempt me to my doom? Shall I kill the king while he's praying, risking that he might go straight to heaven, thereby cheating me of my revenge?" All of these choices seem convincing. They seem like real choices as we sit in the audience.

But we know that they are not. We know that it's a kind of fraud which we willingly allow to be perpetrated on us. We give ourselves over to this fraud because it appears to be the only way to enjoy the play.

But if we are students of theatre craft, we will probably be aware of the wires that make everything work, the lighting and the design of the sets, and we won't necessarily find the story very convincing at all. We only have to take a small step back from involvement in the play to see that of course Hamlet doesn't really have any choice at all. When he comes across the king at his prayers and decides not to plunge his sword into his miserable neck because he does not want to dispatch him to heaven, we know it's ridiculous. There is no individual there. There is nobody who is going to kill and nobody who is going to be killed. We can see through all of that.

The switch from being asleep to being awake is like the switch from the member of the audience caught up in the play to the student of stage craft who has taken a step back from it and has the awareness that Hamlet is an actor going through a routine. There is no choice, no indecision, no meaning, no relationship.

This is only a metaphor of course. I'm trying to suggest that although there can be a very persuasive appearance of choice and of a separate individual, it is sometimes very easy to see through it as in the case of a character in a play.

Seeing through a persuasive appearance is all that we're talking about here. But until it is seen through, there is a very convincing display going on of meaning, purpose, individuality, separateness and choice. "Will I fulfil my destiny or won't I? Will I live a good life or a bad life?"

When this is finally seen through, in a way it destroys everything. Seeing through the appearance is the great destroyer of illusion. It cuts through everything. It cuts through all the stories. Of course non-duality is also a story but it's the mother of all stories, the story to end all stories, because it cuts through all of the others.

Everything is shouting at us "You are an individual and you can make your life work." From advertising hoardings to pulpits, from "This hair shampoo will transform your life" to "This religion will transform your life" there is a babble of voices insisting "You are a person and you can make your life work – particularly if you do whatever I suggest." We are surrounded by exhortations to do something more, to become something else, to be something other than what we are right now, exhortations insisting that this, as it is, isn't enough. On our death bed, at the age of ninety-six, there may still be a voice insisting that in our entire ninety-six years there wasn't a single moment of 'this is it', that there was always something more that we should have been doing to make our life work.

Many of these exhortations sound very heroic. Nikos Kazantzakis, the author of 'Zorba the Greek', wrote as his own epitaph that we should leave to death only a burned out castle. This sounds very noble and rich and redolent with life's surging energy. Live life to the full! There's a part of me that thinks that it's lovely. But it's another exhortation. Even in this, there are so many assumptions; firstly that there is somebody who could choose to do this, secondly that it is meaningful to do this, thirdly that it's better to do this, fourthly that you may have failed as a human being and you may be inadequate if you don't do this. There is that sense behind every exhortation to live your life in a certain way: "If you don't, you have failed."

Perhaps this afternoon we can consign all exhortations to the rubbish bin and suggest instead that there is nothing that needs to be done, there is nothing that needs to be achieved and there is no inadequacy. It is possible that sitting here it may be seen that not only is this all there is, but that this is enough. Hearing that

146

my life has no more meaning than a flower (and no less) might produce a sigh of relief and some relaxation.

If we just sit and relax into this without any suggestion that we should do something, as a result of that we might feel happier.

I'd take the 'as a result' out of that. This is enough and in this happiness may arise. Within Tibetan Buddhism, for example, there is the teaching of specific techniques to enable us to become happier. I'm not suggesting that there is anything wrong with these. For a person who feels a lack and who wishes to get somewhere where that lack is felt less, these techniques can be effective. They can induce a feeling of additional well-being. So then you have a person who has practised Tibetan Buddhist techniques and who feels a higher level of well-being, but you still have a person.

You're not saying that there's anything wrong with doing a technique to become happier?

No, I'm not, any more than I'm suggesting that there's any one who can make a choice about doing it. There's nothing wrong with it, it may be felt to be helpful, but in a sense we could regard it as another oppression, as the suggestion that there is something else that we're failing at. "You are inadequate in your level of happiness and you should be doing something about that."

If we're just sitting, allowing the mind to chatter, listening to the mind, it might come up with all sorts of misleading things for us to do.

I'd go further than that. I'd say that it's almost inevitable that the mind will do that. Then it will either be listened to or it won't. I'm not suggesting that there's anyone who can choose whether to listen to it and I'm not suggesting that there's any technique we can practise to make it any less likely that the mind will be listened to. The mind in any case will usually distort any message it hears into a message about individuality, choice, effort, process, getting somewhere, moving forward in time towards some desired state or moving forward in time away from some undesired state. The two chief energies that create all this drama for a person are the mind's desire to seek satisfaction and its desire to avoid pain. These are the main opposing magnetic energies that bring all of this into life.

It's possible that if the mind beats its head against the brick wall of non-duality for long enough, it might start to give up. But you shouldn't take that as a suggestion that there's a method here – that we can get our mind to abandon itself by going to enough of these talks. Nevertheless that can simply happen. Through being immersed in this communication, the mind can get tired of the frustration of getting nowhere and give up.

Is it helpful if we dedicate our daily activities to the service of God?

No. No one will be blessed by dedicating their day to the service of God and no one will be cursed for not doing so.

There may be two individuals. One offers up their day to the service of God and the other does not. You've still got two people, one of whom is doing one thing and the other another. What we're talking about here is seeing through all of that, seeing that there is no one who can offer anything up to God and no God to whom this non-existent person can offer anything. But until that's seen, the apparent choice to dedicate my day to God may seem very meaningful. It may make perfect sense within the story and will probably be accompanied by many moral judgements about worthiness and unworthiness.

One of the most shocking things that may be seen in awakening is that every concept I have about morality is rendered meaningless. This is very offensive to many individual minds. "How can courage, honesty, integrity, sincerity, selflessness, service to others, be meaningless! What are you talking about!" We can hear how offensive this sounds to an individual who feels there are choices to be made.

(Laughing) In some ways this communication can be heard as terrible, as a wasteland, a desert.

If all this arises in being –

There's no 'if' about it, but go on.

If this is all there is, you could say that all this is arising in God. Then I can dedicate my day to God. If I find that helpful, couldn't I do that, seeing God as no different to non-duality? Or will that interfere with my pursuit of Oneness?

As long as there's the sense of a person there, it may appear that you are offering up your life to the service of God. That may be conceptualised as no different to what is being said here about non-duality, Oneness. And there may also be the concept that this might or might not interfere with your pursuit of non-duality. But what I'm saying is that there is no one who is pursuing non-duality.

There's nothing wrong with what you're saying. There's also nothing right with it. It's simply a set of concepts about actions which appear to be happening. It seems as if there's an individual, an entity with volition. There's no entity, there's no volition, but if these concepts arise, they arise. They're no more and no less meaningful than the cup of tea which we may drink in about twenty minutes' time. There's no one who can do anything about them and there's nothing that needs to be done about them. They don't matter. They're not going to be a hindrance and they're not going to be a help. But if they're thought to be helpful by the person, they will probably be pursued.

Isn't it confusing to start adding the word 'God' to non-duality?

It probably is. But that doesn't matter.

If there's someone who feels that their day is made meaningful through service to God, that's just another phenomenon. There's the sensation of fingers holding a coffee cup, the taste of coffee, the thought that this day is dedicated to God, the sound of a car going past. These are all simply phenomena arising in presence, undifferentiated being manifesting as difference.

I'm not suggesting that moral precepts need to be given up. There is no one who can give them up. But in awakening, they might give you up.

There's nothing right or wrong with them?

There's nothing right or wrong with them but they do create a lot of drama. The five acts of 'Hamlet' couldn't unfold without moral precepts, if Hamlet didn't feel that it was a morally good thing to avenge the death of his father. They are necessary for much of the story. Nevertheless they may be seen through.

We have an addictive need for meaning. Meaning often accretes around a moral sense about whatever is felt to be noble or ignoble.

All you have to do is move back one inch and then you can see through the play. Then the play can be enjoyed even more. Before that, fear controls everything.

The story is sustained by the twin desires to move towards pleasure and to avoid pain. They are like the opposite poles of a magnet. Fear, vulnerability, wanting to avoid that which threatens me, is only half the story. The other half is seeking for pleasure, fulfilment and happiness. They are both equally important in keeping the balls in the air, in keeping the juggling act going.

The trouble with metaphors is that they have a tendency to break down if you push them too far. In my earlier metaphor about a play, I wasn't suggesting that once we've seen through it we can't enjoy it any more. When the stories are seen through it's quite possible that this will be enjoyed more, not less, because it's seen to be enough. Life is seen to have enough juiciness of its own so it doesn't need stories with added meaning to make it juicy. 'Life – Now With New Added Meaning' becomes unnecessary. And like the scientifically plausible but actually useless new ingredient in your hair shampoo, you may realise that 'Life's New Added Meaning' was always a fraud anyway.

Just as we sometimes get fed up with our hair shampoo and change it, we sometimes get jaded with life and revive our interest by changing the meaning we attach to it. We might meet someone who persuades us to become a Zen Buddhist or to give up our job as an accountant and become a traveller. Suddenly we've got 'Life with New Added Meaning' and we feel happy and fulfilled because we have a new goal and we have hope again. For a while. Then when we feel jaded with being a Zen Buddhist, we might meet a friend who's become a Catholic priest so we try Catholicism for a time. Other people are often very eager to persuade us to follow their own preferred story because that confirms their faith in it.

So life is like a hair shampoo with new added ingredients occasionally to perk us up?

Yes. And the added ingredients, or meanings, are usually a fraud. But when the person drops away, life itself is enough.

There seems to be a long tradition of thinking that the ego is an impediment to liberation.

The word 'ego' is confusing because we can mean different things by it. The idea that it's an impediment can be heard as very moralistic. It suggests that the ego is a bad thing, that somehow we need to crush it and become selfless and humble. That is not the case at all.

The difference between being asleep and being awake could be thought of as the difference between being a person and being a character. In some ways they're the same, in some ways different. Before liberation, liking toast and Marmite. After liberation, liking toast and Marmite. Before liberation, believing I have choice and volition and I can pursue life purpose and act causally on the world. After liberation, seeing through all of that. That's a big difference, but liking toast and Marmite will probably stay the same.

Likes and dislikes, preferences, will probably still arise as before but not for anybody. They could be seen as the workings of the ego but they don't matter.

****

I've brought along something to read to you today. It's an extract from 'The Listener', the memoirs of a San Fransisco psychoanalyst called Allen Wheelis. He's describing going for a walk with his dog, Monty.

"If then I bend over and pick up a stick, he is instantly before me. The great thing has now happened. He has a mission ... It never occurs to him to evaluate the mission. His dedication is solely to its fulfillment. He runs or swims any distance, over or through any obstacle, to get that stick. And, having got it, he brings it back: for his mission is not simply to get it but to return it. Yet, as he approaches me, he moves more slowly. He wants to give it to me and give closure to his task, yet he hates to have done with his mission, to again be in the position of waiting.

For him as for me, it is necessary to be in the service of something beyond the self. Until I am ready he must wait. He is lucky to have me to throw his stick. I am waiting for God to throw mine. Have been waiting a long time. Who knows when, if ever, he will again turn his attention to me, and allow me, as I allow Monty, my mood of mission?"

I think that's very relevant. Allen is a person. It sounds like Monty is as well. Allen needs meaning in his life and he hasn't got it. As a person, we all need someone to throw us our stick. We see people chasing their sticks out there in the world, sometimes in very satisfying ways. Some sticks are wonderful. They go flying through the air for a whole lifetime. Often these are the more metaphysical sticks, the religious sticks and the spiritual sticks. We scamper after them, our tails wagging.

152

Some of them are boomerangs.

Yes, some of them are boomerangs and they come back and knock us out.

Many beliefs acknowledge unity at their heart.

At the core of many spiritual traditions is the understanding that All is One. But then the mind comes in and immediately says "Yes, All is One, but nevertheless I'm an individual and I can do something to find this." That's where the confusion and the paths start from. So at the root is 'All is One', but the next step is a denial of this. It's a leap to the contrary, back into the sense that I am a person who not only can do something purposive to find Oneness but has to do something purposive. "I'm a person, so in order to see that 'All is One', I've got to do something."

The three Abrahamic religions differ from this because they don't have 'All is One' at their centre. Instead they hold that God is eternally separate from us, so their basic conception remains dualistic, except in their less well-known mystical forms.

These religions lend themselves very well to the development of purposive stories. They insist right from the beginning on duality, not on unity, because they say that there is God and there is the individual and the two must be forever separate. The best the individual can do is to worship God, to approach God, to get close to God, but never to merge with God. So there is always separation in these three religions. This is true of their exoteric forms but not necessarily of their mystical forms, their esoteric forms.

From this idea of eternal separateness from God, it is extremely easy for a purposive story to emerge about what the individual must do in order to approach God and to please him. "Follow the Ten Commandments, be nice to your neighbours, kill lots of heathens" for example.

We could say that these religions all have an internal logic. They hold that we are a separate individual. We must do something to get close to God, but we will always be separate from him.

153

If we please God, our reward will be that we can worship him forever. This is logically consistent and consistently dualistic.

The paths that come out of the apprehension that there is only Oneness are often more contradictory. First they hold that All is One. Then they tell us that we are a separate individual and we have to do something about becoming One. This is just about as contradictory as it's possible to get. Out of this contradiction come all the practices and techniques that it is claimed will get us back to Oneness.

On a psychological and emotional level a lot of these practices are very beneficial for a person. Practising mindfulness for fifteen years, for example, is likely to be very good for us. So it's not surprising that they're very attractive. And now they've merged in some ways with psychotherapeutic practices, some of which are also very good at making the person feel better. But the spiritual practices are presented as having the ability to merge us back into Oneness, whereas the psychotherapeutic techniques usually are not. They are presented as being able to make us feel better once we've expressed our anger towards our mother and forgiven her, for example.

There are two things it might be helpful to remember about non-duality. It's very difficult to communicate and it's very easy to misunderstand. An attempt may be made to communicate it. This attempt will usually be misunderstood. A religion or a spiritual path may then develop around the misunderstanding.

That's what produces the delightful richness, the Bayeux tapestry, of many of the stories.

The Buddha himself said that it was impossible to communicate this. Just to confirm the paradox of timelessness, perhaps we should say that the Buddha, who never existed, made an attempt to communicate that which could not be communicated and was misunderstood, even though there was no one to misunderstand him.

It's said the Buddha was sitting under the bodhi tree when suddenly all was revealed –

Or rather, when Nothing was revealed.

When he saw Nothing, was that in the story or outside the story?

There is only Nothing in which everything arises. The everything that arises is not different to the Nothing. Sitting here, it may be noticed that there is always silence, even though there isn't. It's a paradox. It can't be explained or justified in any logical sense. But it can be noticed.

It may be noticed that there is only silence. If you look at me and say "You seem to be coming out with a lot of chatter", I will say "That chatter is silence making a noise."

There is an absolute difference between noticing noise and noticing that noise is rooted in silence.

****

Who is the watcher in your metaphor of a play? Who suspends their disbelief and gets drawn into the play? If we don't suspend our disbelief and get drawn in, is that what some people mean by the watcher? Is noticing the watcher a sign of spiritual development?

Some people talk about 'witness consciousness'. It's a distancing from the feeling that I am very solidly a person and the development of an awareness which seems to watch myself. It seems as if I am watching or observing life rather than engaged with it. In some of the spiritual paths, this is considered to be a stage in a process leading towards enlightenment. It is a kind of separation between that part of myself which is aware and that part of myself which acts in the world.

Sometimes I become aware of a part of me that watches everything.

Sometimes it's described as detachment. In your case it could just be psychosis. *(Laughter)*

155

Actually, if you hear descriptions of what is called witness consciousness and then you hear descriptions given by people who are going into the initial stages of a psychotic state, they sometimes sound similar.

But witness consciousness is not a necessary stage. There are no stages. In other words, for the person to drop away, they don't first have to separate from themself and stand six inches to their left.

9

Playing Bridge With The Dead

The first thing to say is that what we're here to talk about this afternoon is completely impersonal, whether we call it Oneness, awareness, liberation or non-duality. This communication has nothing to do with me, nothing to do with the individual that's sitting here. If you have heard others talk about non-duality, you've probably noticed that the flavour of the communication changes depending on the nature of the particular character who is sitting here. But if what's being communicated is pure non-duality, then it's only the flavour that changes. One individual might be more serious, another individual less serious, but the communication itself doesn't have anything to do with anything that's personal. And if you're ever listening to somebody who seems to be talking about non-duality but suggests that it is personal, then the best thing to do would be to get out of the room as fast as you can.

The problem is that if the one who is sitting here in this chair thinks that what they're talking about has got anything to do with themself as a person, then you can get all sorts of shenanigans and tricky things happening. I received an e-mail recently mentioning a website where you can download a long e-book which is about all the shenanigans that sometimes go on in the guru-devotee relationship. Although it's very badly written it's an excellent reminder of the mischief that often happens once there is any connection made between a communication about liberation and the individual who is making it. As soon as there is an identification between the individual and the message, so that the individual thinks that the communication has something to do with themself, you can get into all kinds of tricky stuff.

Let me put it another way. I'm sitting here talking about awakening and liberation but this character is neither awakened nor liberated. In fact we can categorically assure ourselves that nobody in this room will ever be awakened or liberated. We could add that there is nobody in this room anyway.

This communication has also got nothing to do with the mind, the understanding or the intellect. So we can talk about this and that has to involve the mind, it has to involve language, but this can be very misleading.

What is the mind?

(Laughing) Oh we're jumping ahead there. Tricky questions coming immediately. Part of the problem about this communication is that everything is paradoxical. I was going to say at some point that I'm using the term 'mind' but actually there is no such thing. So let's come back to that question in a little while.

For the moment let's pretend that there is a mind. For the person there certainly seems to be one and it seems to be a very powerful tool which has enabled me, the person, to do all sorts of things like study for degrees in post-modernism or design houses or learn how to knit or speak French. The mind is certain that having achieved all sorts of wonderful things, it can now lead me, an individual, to liberation. Of course the mind might just stay interested in learning how to speak French, but if it becomes interested in the idea of a spiritual path, spiritual evolution or liberation, it is quite sure that it can get me there. This is a fixation of the mind. There is nothing that it can hear that will dissuade it from this. As long as there seems to be a mind, it will always find a way round any communication that says "Sorry, this is the one area where you are completely redundant." And if the mind hears this and it wants to get a little bit tricky it will go "Right! I will practise making myself completely redundant. I'm going to put myself away in a cupboard and not get involved." Then we have a mind in a cupboard going "Is this working? Is this more like liberation than when I was out in the front room?"

Liberation has got nothing to do with anything the mind can understand. It has nothing to do with the intellect at all. Theoretically we could go out of here with a complete conceptual understanding of non-duality but this has nothing to do with the seeing of non-duality. Meanwhile, there may be someone sitting in a park who's never even heard the words 'liberation' or 'non-duality' and suddenly there may just be sitting in a park with nobody doing it. The mind, as it pops out of its cupboard, is likely to say "That's not fair. I've been following a spiritual path for thirty years and this guy's just been sitting in a park and suddenly he's not there. It's just not fair."

But that is how it is. So understanding this, swapping ideas and concepts about it, can be fun, but it's not the same as seeing liberation. The seeing of liberation is an energetic shift which has nothing to do with any of the things which I may think that I consist of. It has nothing to do with anything that I may conceive myself to be, like the mind, the body, the spirit, the emotions or the chakric system.

Let's come back to that question about the mind. Having spent a little time talking about the mind, here comes the paradox. It does not exist. It is just an idea. There is no such thing as the mind. But there seems to be a mind as long as there's the sense of a person. The mind and the person are almost the same thing, so when the person is seen through, the mind is also seen through. Then what is seen is that the mind, at its simplest, is just a thought. Then it's another thought, followed by another thought. This is as close as we can get to a description of the mind. There is simply the arising of a thought and then its falling away.

159

But where there's the sense of a person, what tends to happen is that thoughts arise so fast and with so much energy connected to them that this creates the appearance that something, a person or a mind, is thinking these thoughts. When much of this energy disappears, then it's seen that the thoughts, the sensations, the perceptions simply arise out of nothing. Actually everything arises out of nothing, thoughts, people, trees, tables. Everything arises out of nothing and falls away again, arises and falls away.

Another way of putting this is that the mind is a process, it's not an entity. The mind is just a process in time – a thought arises and dies, another thought arises and dies. And there is the sensation that there is an entity producing this.

This communication could be about the clearing away of miscon-ceptions.

Yes. But we clear away all the misconceptions and what we have then is a person who has no misconceptions about this anymore. But that's still not the seeing of non-duality.

Is it not possible that as the misconceptions drop away there is a greater availability to experience non-duality? As misconceptions disappear, we may see what is.

Anything's possible, but I detect more than the glimmering of hope for a method in what you're saying. Maybe there's a tech-nique which goes "Gaining clarity about this and clearing all the misconceptions out of the way will bring about the experience of non-duality for me." But you will never see this. This is only seen when 'you' are no longer there.

But if all misconceptions fall away, I might fall away.

As I said, anything is possible and so it's possible that all mis-conceptions could fall away and then the seeing of liberation could arise. But there would be no connection between those two things. There would be no cause and effect at work. We're getting suspiciously close to doing what the mind always wants to do, which is to find a method. The mind cannot believe that there isn't a method. "There must be a method" it says. But there's no teaching being offered here. There are no techniques being suggested here. This is just a communication, an inadequate attempt to try to describe what is, which is all words can ever do. Any character sitting here can only offer an attempt to describe what is, an attempt which is guaranteed to fail. As soon as the character sitting here starts to suggest to you in even the most subtle way that there's a technique which can enable the false person to discover that it is itself false, you should leave even more quickly than if somebody suggests that the seeing of this is personal. No technique is relevant to this, including self-enquiry.

There's quite a strong tendency for the communication, or the miscommunication, of non-duality to be associated with self-enquiry. To the person this seems utterly logical. "If I, using my mind, can peel away the different false conceptions that I have of the self through self-enquiry in order to reveal that there is no unitary self at my core, then surely that must be it! Surely that must reveal liberation!" Not at all. All you have then is a person who has peeled away all the false conceptions of the self and now understands that there is no unitary self at the core. But you still have a person.

Some of us were sunning ourselves on the towpath by the canal this morning talking about how various scientists and quantum physicists are becoming interested in non-duality now. There are people who understand the connections between non-duality and quantum physics, but clearly non-duality has not been seen.

Even self-enquiry will get us nowhere. Perhaps especially self-enquiry will get us nowhere, because this isn't about us getting anywhere.

It sounds confusing to me to say that thoughts just fall away.

We have to use words unfortunately. Well, we don't have to. We could sit here and just drink tea.

This sounds similar to what the Zen masters are talking about.

I'll quote a Zen master. He said to a seeker "I'd like to help you but unfortunately in Zen we don't have anything." That's Zen non-duality. There are some very good sayings among the Zen masters. Another Zen master told his students after a long and arduous meditation retreat "You must be aware that this training may not give you any result whatsoever."

✿✿✿✿✿✿✿✿✿✿

Is liberation necessarily anything to do with a specific event or happening?

Liberation can apparently happen but there's another paradox here because when liberation is seen, it's realised that liberation always was the case. There was never anything that could possibly not have been liberation. This is one of the appalling paradoxes about this. We're in a hopeless case here, where there's no way out, there's no help and there are no techniques.

By the way, if there was a technique, and if there was somebody over here who could suggest to somebody over there that they could do anything, the technique I'd suggest would be "Relax." Just relax. But there's nobody over there who can relax. It's possible that relaxation might take place, but there's no one there who can relax just as there's no one here who could induce relaxation. I wish I could.

But there are techniques which can help you to relax.

Then you've just got a technique that helps you, a person, to relax. So you'll be a relaxed person. There are lots of techniques that will produce relaxed people but they have nothing to do with this. But if there were a technique for this, that might be it.

If there were techniques that worked, I would suggest that you chant the Great Mantra. The Great Mantra is 'Helpless, Hopeless and Meaningless.' I would suggest chanting that and relaxing. But there is nobody who can give up hope, there is no one who can see that they are helpless and, as long as there is a person who finds things meaningful, there is no one who can see that there is no meaning. The person's meaning could be "In ten lifetimes I will be enlightened if I go on clearing my chakras" or it could be "Next year I'll be a wealthy man if I go on studying racing form." It doesn't matter what kind of meaning it is. As long as there's a person who sees meaning beyond the simplicity of this, that meaning can't be given up. So using the mantra 'Hopeless, Helpless and Meaningless' is as futile as anything else.

If in liberation there's just the simplicity of this, where do sensations come from? If they don't belong to you, what are they?

There's still a body-mind organism and sensations go on arising. Phenomena go on happening just as they did before. But it's seen that they are not happening for anyone. This is why anyone making this communication can say quite confidently that we're talking about something quite unexciting here. Seeing through the person, seeing that this is all there is, involves seeing that this is sufficient in itself. It doesn't need any added story or added meaning. This glass of water doesn't need any added meaning for it to be a perfectly satisfactory glass of water and neither does this body-mind organism. Seeing that doesn't seem particularly exciting. If you want excitement, take L.S.D. The phenomena that arise when you take L.S.D. are much more exciting than the seeing of liberation.

So do negative sensations still happen when liberation is seen?

Anything can arise when liberation is seen just as anything can arise when liberation isn't seen. There are no necessary implications in the seeing of liberation. But having said that, there are tendencies for the phenomena that arise to change somewhat. However, they are only tendencies. Negative sensations and positive sensations are both still likely to arise, but it's seen that they don't belong to anybody. There's another paradox here. The difference between phenomena arising for a person and phenomena simply arising is both tiny and cosmic. The mind can't possibly understand this. The mind says "How can it be both tiny and cosmic! That's nonsense. Come on Richard, it's either one or the other!" That's all the mind can do with this.

The awakening event you describe – did it only last for a moment?

Not even a moment because a moment has duration. How long is a moment? It has a beginning, a middle and an end. That's why the word 'presence' is sometimes used when talking about this, or it's said that "all there is, is this" or "this is it". Words are so difficult. There's not even a moment. A moment has a past and a future contained within it and neither exist in 'this'. So we can't even talk about 'now' because 'now' implies a past that never did exist and a future that never will exist. There is just this. Literally. When I say "This is it" I mean that this is the totality. Of course in this, a thought may arise about a conversation that apparently took place on the towpath of the canal this morning about mysticism and quantum physics. That's a thought arising in this. In a sense what that thought does is reveal to us that time is entirely subjective.

When I say "Time is subjective" I don't mean that when you're visiting your in-laws the clock seems to tick more slowly. I mean that time exists only in consciousness, only in the consciousness of a thought. This sentence is expressing a thought. It apparently takes time to get from the beginning of this sentence to the end of it. But the time in which this sentence started never existed and the time in which this sentence will end never will exist. Yet, in subjective consciousness, in awareness, there is the appearance of this thought, which can apparently only take place over time. Another way of grasping this is to go outside and watch a bird fly across the sky. That bird flying across the sky is a miracle, because it defies the non-existence of time. That bird can only fly across the sky because consciousness exists outside time. It is consciousness that constructs time.

Even in a flash of awakening, one of the things that may be seen through is time. Time is seen through quite easily, actually. Of course, we could demonstrate logically that there is no time, that this hall as it existed two seconds ago no longer exists and as it will exist in the next second doesn't exist yet, but there's little point in doing that. These are just concepts to entertain the mind. Nevertheless, in awakening time may simply be seen through. Of course there are no rules about this, no rules at all.

You're talking about awakening as a kind of event and I'm quite comfortable that some people have this event –

Apparently.

Apparently. But surely this seeing through time has been done throughout the ages. Poets for example have seen through time but they wouldn't describe themselves as being awakened. There's no need to lust after this event. And human beings have made up stories about meaning for as long as there have been human beings.

Definitely.

There have always been stories about meaning. It just sounds like you're saying "Oh, I've seen through this meaning."

Not 'I'.

Are you saying that all these stories about meaning are meaning-less? Is that the paradox? You're saying that everything is without meaning and yet within the human condition everyone's experience is pregnant with meaning.

Within a person's experience, yes, it is.

But that's who we are, persons. It's not imaginary at all. Human beings experience meaning.

As long as there's a person, there will be stories about meaning. One way of describing a human being is a 'Meaning-Seeking Missile'. The apparent mind is desperate for meaning and will construct it in a myriad ways. While there's a person it's not possible to see through that, except conceptually. In other words it's possible for a person to construct a philosophy that sees through the stories of meaning. Phenomenology, existentialism and post-modernism are all philosophies that attempt in different ways to deconstruct meaning. But that has nothing to do with what I'm talking about. That's a person in the guise of a philosopher deconstructing meaning. It's a person making up a story about how all the other stories are just made-up stories. But when the person is seen through, the stories simply drop away. Then there's no need to construct yet another story about how all the stories are meaningless. Instead, they're just seen through.

Are you saying that post-modernism is insignificant?

(Laughing) I didn't say that. Ah, another idea I wish I hadn't introduced! I'm simply saying that it's another story and it purports to see through all the older stories, the religious stories, the historical stories, the scientific stories, the stories of human progress. It's another set of concepts and so it doesn't have anything to do with what we're talking about here. If we had a phenomenologist sitting here we might have a lot of agreement about the concepts being exchanged here. We might agree for example that there is no central or unitary self but it would just be agreement on an intellectual level. It would have nothing to do with what we're talking about.

But being in a story is the human condition for most of us. It might be a marvellous thing to see through it but we can't do anything about it.

No, we can't. It's a bit of a mystery that we're sitting here talking about it at all, isn't it?

166

****

Richard, I'd like to come at this from a slightly different angle. In your book you refer to a search and you say that you attended many meetings about this. I've attended many meetings of this sort as well. You had almost reached an impasse. You were still searching but you'd reached an impasse and then something significant happened and now you are sitting here talking to us today.

But it didn't happen to me. That's the point. For the first time in thirty years of seeking something happened but not to me. Actually nothing happened but this is the only way to try to describe it. Are you suggesting there's a causal connection between that and attending meetings like these?

No. What I'm saying is that as an individual I represent possibly hundreds of thousands of people who are in the situation you were in and something happened that triggered off a change that means that you're sitting here talking to us today. What was this highly significant change? Can you explain it?

When you say "explain it" do you mean describe it or give a cause for it?

From my understanding of your book you had reached an impasse – I'm not saying you'd given up –

It's not possible to give up.

No, but you'd exhausted your understanding and then something happened. Could you elaborate on that? There are many people who might have the same question.

There are no rules about this but there were what I describe as two events. The word 'event' is a way of avoiding the word 'experience' because for me an experience is something that happens to a person. So there were two events, one of which was instantaneous – it lasted half a second or a second – where there was the complete disappearance of the person. A phrase that comes to me in trying to describe this is one that is sometimes used by Buddhists. They talk about seeing the emptiness of all phenomena or sometimes they speak of empty phenomena rolling by. I describe this as awakening because there is a momentary seeing that there is no one here, no self, no person, no individual. But after that momentary event the person tends to come back. That is what happened in this story here. So then there's a memory of this event and all sorts of changes might take place as a result of it but essentially the person has come back and will probably still be searching. There can then be a period of what's sometimes called being in a desert, a period of desolation. Particularly if you were a spiritual seeker, what's often seen in that awakening event is that all the methods, all the hanging around with gurus, all the clearing of chakras, all the receiving of shaktipat, all the darshans and the aura cleansing, are totally irrelevant. The trouble is that after awakening, the person who feels themself to be separate is still there and because they still feel separate, they still feel dissatisfied and therefore they are still seeking.

(Laughing) By the way, we'll be doing shaktipat after tea.

So now there's a person who's still dissatisfied and still seeking but who knows that there's no valid method of seeking. There's also a 'memory' of this event which seemed to make everything clear but it's now gone. It can be quite a desperate place, although I'm not saying it is for everyone. What happened here was that the person came back and misunderstood this event. The person who came back thought "Wow. That's it!", because in that emptiness it was seen that there was clearly an end to any possibility of personal suffering. There was no person there and this emptiness felt incredibly attractive. There was then an assumption that if I waited there would be more of that and eventually it would become a permanent state.

Later on there was another longer event when the person again disappeared. After that the sense of a contracted individual didn't come back. That was over. What was also realised was that the emptiness which had been seen is a full emptiness.

Are you happier now?

(Laughing) If I uttered the words "*I* am happier now" I would be burnt as a heretic by the Convocation of Non-Duality Bishops. *I* am not happier now because there is no I.

Does happiness arise more often there? (Laughter)

Any phenomena which occurred before could still happen. Increased happiness could arise but not for anybody. But there are no necessary implications in this and there's nothing to be gained by anyone in this. Having said that, I have noticed that there is a tendency for the phenomena that arise to be somewhat different. For example, there is a tendency for neurotic feelings to lessen although not necessarily to die away completely. I make a distinction between natural feelings and neurotic feelings. Natural feelings are feelings like anger, sadness, fear and happiness. But there are a great many other feelings that can arise which I call neurotic feelings. For example, guilt, irritation, anxiety, embarrassment and self-consciousness are all neurotic feelings.

These neurotic feelings could be thought of as originating in natural feelings but the person gets in the way of them and interferes with them. For example anger simply arises as a natural feeling, but if there's a neurotic person there they may get in the way of the anger being fully felt. So instead of feeling five minutes of anger, we might feel five days of irritation. There are many people who suffer from I.B.S. That stands for 'Irritable Brain Syndrome'. Some people can walk around being irritable for twenty years. That's a neurotic manifestation of anger which can happen when a person gets in the way of the pure feeling simply being felt. Be aware that this is all a story, but the point I'm making is that when liberation is seen there is a tendency for neurotic feelings to lessen. That could mean that natural feelings increase. Instead of a week's irritation there might be ten minutes of anger. I'm not going to say whether that's better or worse. But the idea that this is about constant peace, bliss and harmony is ludicrous.

If you want constant bliss, you could try taking heroin, but I don't recommend it.

But I do want bliss! And I don't want to take heroin!

Well, your best hope for this afternoon is that you get Nothing out of it.

Is your character attached to what you're speaking about?

No, my character doesn't give a damn.

Are you attached to your way of speaking about this?

No.

Can you speak about it in a different way?

Yes. But I'm not going to. I could do the rest of the afternoon in broken French but I don't see any point in that. Please, somebody, anybody, ask another question! *(Laughter)*

I have a really difficult question. Even though in your case there's been liberation –

Not 'in my case'.

Nevertheless, what's left of your mind-body is partaking in this conversation and evidently enjoys the sharing of liberation –

What do you mean by 'the sharing of liberation'?

It's like you've come back to tell us the story.

(Laughing) Like Lazarus raised from the dead?

So if there's nobody there, what's left? What's telling the story?

The body-mind organism is left. But what's telling the story is Oneness. Oneness is here and Oneness is over there. Oneness is talking to Oneness. Liberation is talking to liberation. There is only liberation. The sense of a separate individual who may feel very unliberated and who thinks "I need another twenty years of clearing my chakras" is also liberation. It's liberation expressing itself as the feeling of not being liberated.

Oneness is talking to Oneness and Oneness is listening to Oneness. In the play, in the appearance, it clearly sometimes amuses Oneness to listen to itself talking about itself. Most of the time it doesn't. Most of the time it amuses Oneness to go out and get drunk or watch football or start wars or build churches or go to the latest fashion show or save the planet. These are clearly what amuse Oneness most of the time but occasionally Oneness likes to listen to itself hearing itself talking about itself.

Talking about non-duality is also a story. Anything that can be put into words is a story. So what we are gathered here today to talk about is the story of non-duality. It's not the story of Islam or Christianity or Buddhism but it's still a story. I would make one distinction however. There is no difference in what we're doing here today from what we might be doing at a fashion show or at a Christian church service except that the story we are telling this afternoon is the story which points to reality as it is in the most direct manner. Most of the other stories add fantastical decorations and curlicues on top of what actually is. That's the only difference in what we're doing here this afternoon. For no particular reason, Oneness occasionally decides that it would like to listen to itself talk about itself in as clear a way as possible, to get as close as words can actually get to reality, rather than listening to all the decorative curlicues that are usually added on top. By decorative curlicues, I mean such stories as the world religions, the spiritual paths, the guru stories, anything which is a more complicated story than "This is it, folks. And if this doesn't seem to be enough, tough, because this is all there is."

But the person hears this and tends to say "But it's not enough! There's got to be more!" That's when all the other stories start. The stories start from "It can't just be this! It can't just be the simple drinking of this glass of water!" Then they might go on to "Life has to be an exam in which I have to prove that I can please God and at the end of it I die and I go to heaven. And when I'm in heaven I can laugh at all my enemies who didn't please God and consequently are in hell." That's what the person may say because for the person this isn't enough. But when the person isn't there anymore, it's not only seen that "This is it" but it's also seen that "This is it and this is sufficient." This is fascinating enough in itself. This glass of water is a miracle. We don't need the Roman Catholic Church to declare miracles. This is already a miracle.

The church doesn't get many miracles these days!

I'm not an expert.

Would it make sense to say that Oneness has a sense of humour?

Everything that arises is a manifestation of Oneness. So humour and tragedy are both manifestations of Oneness.

So is humour a characteristic of Oneness?

Any phenomenon is a manifestation of Oneness – including humour.

There is only Oneness. So anything that you can mention is Oneness manifesting as whatever is.

So how would you describe its purpose or intention?

It has no purpose or intention.

What about evil?

Evil is a judgement made by the mind. The believer burns the heretic. The heretic allows themself to be burned for their heretical beliefs. One person's highest good is another person's deepest evil.

It leads us down an even more misleading path than words are already leading us down to start ascribing qualities to Oneness. Everything is a manifestation of Oneness. There's nothing else anything could possibly be. As soon as you start excluding anything, you're back in the world of duality. This is something the mind finds very tough. There are all sorts of things that the mind sees going on out there which it doesn't like and wants to exclude. The mind says "That can't be part of Oneness." As soon as the mind says that, we're back in duality. Because now we've got Oneness and we've also got the stuff that we've excluded from it, that we've put outside it. "What about war? War can't possibly be part of Oneness!" So now we're back in duality. We've got Oneness and we've also got something that is separate from it.

The mind always sees duality.

****

I've got the sense that words always fail to capture this.

Yes, they have to fail.

What about all the time I've spent doing spiritual practices?

I still teach meditation. I've been teaching meditation for thirty years.

So it's not a waste of time to meditate?

Meditation can be a wonderful thing to do. It just doesn't have anything to do with what we're talking about here. I put meditation and many other techniques into a box called 'making the prison more comfortable'. Of course, really there is no one who is in a prison. But as long as there is a sense that we are in a prison, it's a very good idea to do what we can to make that prison more comfortable. Certain things are much better at doing this than others. Meditation is a better way of making the prison more comfortable than drinking lots of whisky.

I find whisky more effective. (Laughter)

O.K. Whisky can be pretty good as well. Psychotherapy can be a very effective way of making the prison more comfortable. But psychotherapy has nothing to do with seeing liberation. It's quite likely that psychotherapy and meditation may produce a person who is more comfortable in their perceived prison. But they will still be a person in a perceived prison. When the person drops away, not only is it seen that there isn't a person in the prison, it's seen that there never was a prison in the first place. Because the prison is the sense of being a person. When the sense of being a person isn't there anymore there's no possibility of there being a prison.

There isn't always a person though, is there?

No.

In your book you talk about dying, but we die all the time that we have no self-awareness. We come back every now and then and realise we've been thinking but we're virtually unconscious a lot of the time.

Yes, we're often 'on automatic'.

And as I understand it, that's no different to death. The big difference with death is that you don't come back afterwards because there's no nervous system to identify as a person.

The difference between being on automatic and physical death is that there are phenomena arising in the first.

Sometimes there's awareness that there's a person and sometimes there isn't. Sometimes there's an awareness of little things, sometimes there's an awareness of mystical experiences. All this is dependent on having a nervous system. The difference, as I understand it, is it's said that in liberation awareness is aware of itself. There's no evidence for this that I can understand.

No, there can't be any evidence for this until it is seen. And then it's just obvious. There's nothing more I can say about that. When the person drops away then it's simply seen.

But when the person drops away, you're just carrying on doing things.

You're not. But there is still awareness of things being done and actions being taken. Phenomena still arise. It's simply seen that there is no one who is doing any of that. So phenomena don't change. But the sense of contraction ends. The sense of being a separate contracted person who has to negotiate with life, who seeks pleasure and avoids pain, the sense of that person collapses.

But that sense is only there sometimes anyway. I don't see how this is an elevated state in any way.

It's not an elevated state. All we're talking about here ultimately is the natural state of being.

But that's totally independent of people.

Everything's totally independent of people.

So what's the point of people?

There is no point to people. There's no point to anything. That's The Great Mantra. 'Hopeless, Helpless and Meaningless.' Seeing through purpose and meaning is absolutely core to this. But I don't mean that you can do that and that might get you somewhere. It's the other way round. When this is seen, purpose and meaning and point fall away, taking all the stories with them.

There has to be an awareness that is completely independent of anything.

175

Yes. Awareness is completely independent of everything. Awareness does not require phenomena.

Is it aware of itself? Is it not aware only because there are people who have sensations? Does it not need nervous systems?

It doesn't need anything but obviously there seems to be some kind of delight in experiencing phenomena. That is why a word that is used for this in the Eastern tradition is 'lila'. Let's settle on 'play' as a translation of that. This is a story, a drama, an entertainment. That's as close as we can get to describing it. There is no point to people and there is no purpose to life but if we want to get as close as we can to answering the question "What is going on?" it's an entertainment. It's a play. It's 'Hamlet'. Or you could call it a dream. It's Oneness dreaming that it is Hamlet dreaming that he really is a prince in Denmark.

It's a pretty mean entertainment if it's only enjoyed by a few in the audience.

As long as there is the sense of being a person, there will be a sense of personal suffering. So sometimes this can seem pretty vicious. So can 'Hamlet' if you get caught up in it. When that sword goes through Polonius's guts behind the arras –

I put books like that down.

But you can be watching the play and if it's a good production you'll be caught up in it. And this is a very good production. Look how real it seems. Look at these props *(tapping the wall)*, these painted sets which have nothing behind them. Look at those hills through that window. Don't they look real to you? Look at how three-dimensional they seem. This is a very good production, so it's hardly surprising that we get sucked into it. We suspend our disbelief and end up thinking we are characters in the play. Some of us think that we're courtiers, some of us think that we're Hamlet.

That's the best we can say about what seems to be going on. I know that to the mind this is unsatisfactory, but it's less unsatisfactory than any other story. It gets a bit closer to describing this than the other stories do. One of the reasons it's unsatisfactory is that nothing is actually going on anyway. Most of what we have been talking about is predicated on the idea that there is time and that something is happening. But there isn't any time and nothing is happening. There's only this.

It seems easy to understand that 'me' is just an idea and then another idea and then another idea. It's also easy to see that time is created by the mind and that the mind itself is an apparition. But there seems to me to be a massive gap between understanding that and identifying myself with the awareness that is manifesting as me and as you and as everything else. There is no way that I can do that.

That's the whole point. There is no way that *you* can do that. There is no way that you can do anything about that as long as there is this sense of being a separate person. But when contraction becomes expansion, when there is that energy shift, then this is seen. It's either seen while there's a body-mind or it's seen at death. It doesn't matter which. It will seem to the person that it does matter, but it doesn't. "At death there is only liberation. It's just more chic to see liberation while you're alive." But that's not how it feels to a person.

Why is there a resistance to seeing this in the individual?

You could say that it's necessary for the game to take place. Without that resistance, there wouldn't be this drama. Without contraction into a sense of individuality, the game wouldn't happen. But that is just a story as well. The trouble with 'why' questions is they always imply purpose. But there is no purpose. 'Why' questions seek reasons and what I'm suggesting is there are no reasons. I'm very wary of 'why' questions, but if you want an answer, that's the answer.

177

Could you get our sense of individuality to drop away? All at once? So everybody leaves here as no one?

I wish. I'd charge a lot of money.

Would you really wish that?

I'd love to. Why not? It sounds lovely. Liberation would be seen and everybody would have tea. But you're talking impossibles.

****

Richard, I feel I've had glimpses of what you're talking about but not the complete thing. But I'd describe some of what you're saying as a philosophy. To say that there's no purpose might be correct or it might not. When the universe ends we might say "Richard was right", but I feel life will probably carry on developing indefinitely and exploration will go on forever. Over the next few millennia we might discover all sorts of things and one of them might be that there is a purpose. So are you one hundred per cent certain of what you're saying?

I'm not. Of course not. This communication has nothing to do with me.

Do you think there's a chance that your interpretation could be slightly askew?

This is not an interpretation or a philosophy. This is simply seen and there's nothing philosophical in that. It's just seen that this is it in its entirety. There is no meaning or purpose beyond what is. What's more, there doesn't need to be. It makes no more sense to say that this person has a purpose than to say that the tree out there in the garden blowing in the breeze has a purpose. We don't look at the tree and ask "Is that tree fulfilling its purpose? Is it being a good tree? Is it evolving towards the highest level of spiritual evolution that a tree can reach?"

It appears that you and others like you who talk about non-duality agree that there is no purpose.

Do you think that's suspicious? *(Laughter)*

Has it ever occurred to you nevertheless that you could be fooling yourself?

You're personalising the communication. I started off by saying that this communication is completely impersonal and I advised you to leave the room if it wasn't. There's nothing personal about this and it isn't a philosophy. It's simply a description of what remains when the person is gone and when it's seen that all the stories and the meanings are made up, all the purposes are invented.

That's what the mind does. It makes up stories. That's what people do and we do it because we feel separate and therefore dissatisfied. We feel dissatisfaction because we have a nagging sense that somehow, somewhere, we've lost something. This is because we really have lost something. As soon as self-consciousness occurs, we lose the sense of unity. We start living in the world of duality. From that point on we have the sense that "This isn't it. It can't be! There must be something else!" Then a search starts, which may last seventy years, to find that elusive thing which seems to be missing.

We've been searching for thousands of years.

I'm talking about the life of an individual who starts on a search to find whatever will put an end to their sense of dissatisfaction. We look for it everywhere – in money, in relationships, in our children, in our work, in religions, in spiritual paths. We keep looking because since that initial sense of separation we feel there's something missing. That's where all the stories about meaning and purpose come from.

I'm not necessarily disagreeing, but for now I can think of a lot of reasons why you might be wrong.

Of course. The mind always will. The mind will always try to wriggle out of this. It can't help doing that. The mind will say "It can't be that. It's too simple."

You're speaking as if there's a person there. You keep saying 'I' and 'me'.

It sounds paradoxical, but we have to use language that is at least halfway acceptable. We could torture language till its joints cracked to get it closer to what is meant but it becomes impossible to listen to.

The people I've heard giving talks about this have sometimes seemed very different to each other. If the person's gone, why should the teachers have these different personalities?

When the person has been seen through there's still a body-mind with a character. There are still character traits, feelings, preferences and likes and dislikes. Seeing this might make no difference to the personality. Everyone has their own flavour. Some people who talk about this might be humorous and tell jokes, others might be very serious. Some people swear, some are rather ascetic. All of that is just the flavour of the personality. In the same way, the personality of the listener will have a flavour so they will be drawn to one kind of communication rather than another. An ascetic listener will be drawn to an ascetic communicator and might shun one who swears.

Sometimes I've heard talks about non-duality where the ideas being presented sounded radically different.

If you look at the many people who say that they are talking about non-duality, a lot of them are actually talking about something else. Often they are presenting a story of an evolving personal spiritual path but couched in the language of non-duality. At its heart will be the suggestion that they have got somewhere which you haven't yet reached and they can teach you something which will help you to get there as well.

I'd be very wary of that message.

If you consider humanity as a whole, it's obvious that the individual is not going to evolve, but humanity as a whole may.

You say it's obvious, but the idea of individual evolution is at the root of most spiritual paths.

Can you really say that there is no evolution?

Yes. But you're quite entitled to throw that in the waste bin. Evolution is something that takes place in time and it's part of a story. In fact it's part of many different stories.

We 'storyify' it. We make up stories about it from moment to moment. That doesn't mean that evolution doesn't exist.

You asked me a question and that's the answer that comes out from here. You and many other people might choose to put it in the waste bin. It doesn't matter.

****

We experience pain in a very personal way. We might be inclined to think "Why me?"
Is there any difference now in how pain is experienced?

The body is the body.

What would you do if I came out and stamped on your foot?

It's too hypothetical. I don't know. I might hit you or go and look for a doctor.
Pain is pain. And what may lie behind a question like yours is

"Surely there must be some reward in this. Surely there's something in it for me." But there isn't any reward for a person.

Suppose I was fighting in a war and I was being tortured. If I wanted to go and fight in a war, one of the things that would prevent me would be the fear of being captured and tortured.

This is getting rather convoluted. "If liberation was seen, would I be able to fight in a war and disregard being tortured?" It's too hypothetical.

It's not hypothetical. Most of the time that we're not experiencing pain, there's just a sort of dullness. We're not on the cutting edge. One of the things that prevents me from putting myself in harm's way is that I don't want to experience pain.

You think that's the case. What I'm suggesting is that this is just what's happening. You think you're causing yourself not to put yourself in harm's way. But you're not. That's just what's happening.

But there'd be a complaint from me if I was being hurt.

Yes, probably. There would be from here as well, I would guess. The body's the body. Pain is pain.

One of the problems with this, arising from our tendency to personalise our fantasy of liberation, is that we can create an idealised image of the guru or teacher. We may think that they must be beyond pain and that they must live in perpetual bliss. Someone once said to me "If you and I were sitting in an aeroplane and it was plunging towards the earth in flames, I'd be screaming but you'd just be calmly sitting there, wouldn't you?" It's a bit hypothetical, but I doubt it. The body-mind has a natural tendency to try to preserve itself. That's just what happens.

But alongside that do you think that in the plunging aeroplane this would still be seen through or would there be a return to contraction?

We want the person in the chair giving the talk to know stuff like that.

One of the ways in which we keep ourselves seeking is to project onto a teacher an ideal of an 'enlightened' person who is so far above us that we can feel we could not reach their state in fewer than twenty lifetimes. We may create an idealised enlightened figure who is above and beyond any thought of pain and any possibility of suffering, who lives in utter bliss, who can perform wonderful siddhis and who can release us from our karma if we only show him enough devotion. There can be a powerful tendency to project this idealised figure out there. The more idealised this teacher is, the more our own search can be kept going.

The search, particularly if it's for spiritual enlightenment, is sustained by our sense of personal inadequacy. Most spiritual paths are sustained by this. "I am not yet good enough but if I follow the guru, repeat the mantra, do enough chanting, clear my chakras and receive darshan often enough, then I will become good enough and one day I will be utterly purified." All spiritual seeking stems from this core sense that "I am not yet adequate." Imagining that there is an idealised teacher out there who is totally adequate maintains our own sense of inadequacy in comparison.

This approach to spirituality seems to be very Eastern.

Most religious and spiritual paths have at their root this belief in inadequacy which can be resolved either through some kind of spiritual evolution or through redemption. This might be through practising spiritual techniques or through salvation by a forgiving God, for example. The core belief is that we are not adequate and there is somewhere else that we need to get to or something else that we need to become.

That says more about the human condition than about religion.

Yes, this is absolutely the human condition. But it is out of the human condition that all the religious and spiritual stories arise.

****

Can you say more about the difference between contraction and localisation?

For an individual there is a sense of contraction, but it isn't usually recognised as such. Until there is an expansion out of it, contraction has always been the case so it can't be recognised. If we were colour blind and we had always seen the grass as grey, how would we know that we were seeing it strangely?

But there is also a sense of localisation which has nothing to do with contraction. It simply has to do with the fact that the phenomena associated with being a person are apparently located over here rather than over there. In the 'events' of awakening and liberation both contraction and localisation ended so there was no sense of either.

So you were nowhere?

I was not. It was simply seen that awareness is everywhere and everything. There was no distinction between this person and this table. There was no space and no time. But that sense of non-localisation doesn't remain. Nathan Gill gives a good description of non-localisation. He was riding a bicycle and then there was just bicycling. Tony Parsons was walking through a park and then there was just walking. But in the story of time the sense of localisation comes back.

But contraction ending must change the feelings that happen after that.

Feelings are feelings. Pain is pain. Anger is anger. The person is often very good at attenuating suffering. They may have a lot of ways of turning down the volume of suffering. When contraction ends and the person isn't there anymore, instead of nervousness, for example, which is all the person may be allowing to ripple through to consciousness, there may be a heightened sense of fear. But it's just fear. It's just a phenomenon.

Things might be more intense but they might be over more quickly?

Certainly feelings might be over more quickly. A person often has so many ways of protecting themself against the intensity of feelings. This is a point on which psychotherapeutic insights and non-duality come very close together. For example in some forms of psychotherapy, it is felt that if there is an uncomfortable feeling, one of the most helpful things that we can do is to allow ourself to feel that feeling as fully as possible, to give it our full attention. This is very like the Buddhist technique of mindfulness which is now being used increasingly by mental health professionals because it is so effective. If we really feel the feeling then what happens is it tends to transform. This is quite similar to what may be seen in non-duality. The difference is that in the psychotherapeutic story, it is usually believed – although not always – that there is somebody who can choose to do this. But what I'm saying is that when liberation is seen, there's just a tendency for this to happen. There's a tendency for feelings simply to arise and not be interfered with and then to die away.

****

Does the mind die with the body?

There is no mind so the mind doesn't die with the body.

But mediums communicate with dead people.

Well, I'd say that's proof. So forget what I said about death. *(Laughter)*

How do you explain mediums then?

185

The mind – which does not exist – does not want to contemplate its own annihilation. It also finds it very painful to contemplate the annihilation of loved ones. So when faced with the possibility of annihilation at death, the mind makes up stories about how this is not going to happen. We make up these stories because there is such an attachment to the idea of being an individual who continues forever. Some minds are structured so that they can apparently receive communications from dead aunts who tell them not to worry about death because there'll still be a bridge club on the other side. It's just another phenomenon. It has no more and no less meaning than anything else. A glass of water arises. A communication from dead Aunt Mabel arises.

I don't want to believe that. I don't want to believe I end when I die.

Yes, it's horrible, isn't it. For a person it's terrible. As long as there's an identification with a person it's awful. When that leaves, then it isn't awful anymore.

So do we just merge into one at death?

Everything's already merged into one.

So what about dead Aunt Mabel?

Dead Aunt Mabel is having a bloody good time on the other side. *(Laughter)*

Aunt Mabel is just a phenomenon. There are simply whatever phenomena arise. If I'm sitting here and I'm hearing dead Aunt Mabel's voice in my head then that's the phenomenon that's arising. If there's ectoplasm hovering in the air that looks like Aunt Mabel, it's just a phenomenon. We can't even understand how a cup of tea arises – let's not try to understand Aunt Mabel's ectoplasm. It's a waste of time. Dead Aunt Mabel or this glass of water, it's really the same thing, it's phenomena. Phenomena arise and fall away and we give them meaning. The meaning we give them is also just a phenomenon.

But in the context of the dream, is what the medium says true or false?

There is no true or false within the context of the dream. There are only phenomena arising.

Well, I don't agree that there's nothing behind it.

I wouldn't expect you to. But let's be precise about this. What is the 'it' that you're referring to? What is the phenomenon or the set of phenomena that you're asking about? Are you asking about a medium who channels Aunt Mabel? What's real is that there's the phenomenon of a voice apparently channelling an aunt. 'Real' is a difficult word anyway, but the most sensible way to use it is to describe the phenomena that arise. These are what is real. But you want there to be an Aunt Mabel behind the medium, or at least you'd like that possibility.

Lot's of people want that possibility.

Of course. You bet we do. That's what a person does. All I can add about death is that it'll o.k.

But some people who give talks about non-duality talk about re-incarnation and other lifetimes.

There are a lot of people out there who say that they're talking about non-duality but actually they're not. There have always been people claiming to talk about non-duality but really telling a very complicated story. Now 'however' non-duality is becoming rather the flavour of the month so that's happening more and more. There are plenty of people who say that they're talking about non-duality and then they'll offer you a workshop on how you can discover that you aren't anybody. It's nonsense.

Couldn't you be taken to task for telling a story?

187

It's all a story. As soon as there's self-consciousness we start to tell stories.

Could you say this is simply about life itself?

Yes. Life. Being. Energy. Awareness. None of the words will do but they're all we have.

What about Douglas Harding's experiments to discover that you're not a person? Is that the same sort of thing as you're talking about?

I liked Douglas Harding's approach. I attended one of his evenings many years ago. It's interesting but it still feels quite conceptual. However, it can provoke an 'aha', a realisation that "I am not in this. This is in me." But that's where the 'aha' falls short because although I am not in this, this isn't in me either because there is no me.

If people tried to walk through that wall over there everybody would bang their head. But if I just imagined a wall over there people would walk through it quite happily. Some things within the story appear to be real and some things don't. So are things like spiritualism real or imaginary?

What I mean by 'real' is whatever phenomena are arising. So if somebody goes over there and bumps their head against that wall, that is what has arisen – a bruise on the head. If someone goes into a trance and starts talking in the voice of Aunt Mabel, then what's arising is that somebody has gone into a trance and is speaking in the voice of Aunt Mabel. You may then tell a story which goes "Aunt Mabel is on the other side. She's communicating with me. That suggests that my own sense of personal identity will continue after death." This is the core of that story and the importance of all those kinds of story. As I said, the mind does not wish to contemplate its own annihilation. But when liberation is seen, the mind's annihilation is no longer a problem because it's seen that there is no mind to be annihilated.

You've said there are no choices. I feel I make choices but you say that things just happen. In practice are you saying that events are just like a stream of feelings that flows through me?

There isn't even a stream of feelings. Actually there is nothing happening. But you could say that a stream of events seems to be happening and added to that is the idea "I am choosing to do this".

It just seems like a joke.

It's the greatest joke of all.

So how can I get out of thinking there are choices?

You can't get out of it although you can talk yourself out of believing in choices. Ramesh Balsekar talks people out of believing in choice. He starts with an apparent choice that someone has made and takes the person back through the chain of events that led up to it, demonstrating to them logically that at no point was there any real choice. Their circumstances, their genetic make-up, the family and cultural pressures on them, all made their apparent choice inevitable. But this is just conceptual. It's not really relevant to what we are talking about. As long as there's the sense of a person it will seem that this person is making choices. If the sense of a person falls away, that is seen through. Even then there could still be thoughts of choice arising, but they won't be taken seriously.

Interestingly there has been research recently that strongly suggests that there is also a scientific basis for saying that there is no choice. There have been experiments that show that about a third of a second before we're conscious of making a choice to perform an action, the parts of our brain that are involved in performing that action are already activating. The physical organism gets ready to perform the action before we're conscious of choosing to do it. In other words, before we decide to pick up a pencil, the body is already getting ready to pick up the pencil. This is very challenging to our normal conception of what it is to be a person. There are now many scientists and other thinkers who will strongly argue that there is no possibility of personal choice or free will. For example, many scientists are materialist realists and they might say that there is no room for free choice. But this is just another conceptual story. It has nothing to do with actually seeing that 'I' am not a person.

****

You've talked about emptiness. What about qualities like courage, loyalty and integrity? Are they meaningless?

When the self drops away what can be seen is the emptiness of all phenomena. But what may also be seen is that this is a very full emptiness. What it's full of is love. So the answer to your question about those other qualities is "Yes, they are meaning-less. But everything is unconditional love." There's nothing more I can say to help you make sense of that. All I can say is that when the person is seen through, everything is seen to be love. Within that, qualities such as courage, loyalty and integrity are in a way meaningless because they only make sense if they contain the idea of choice. But there are still going to be preferences in the character after the person has dropped away and the preference may still be for someone who appears to act courageously or with integrity. So it doesn't make any difference. If the person behaved courageously before liberation was seen, it's likely that the char-acter will still behave in the same way afterwards. So other people might say "Oh look, he's quite courageous."

But I think it matters whether people are courageous and have integrity.

For a person things often seem to matter.

So are there no thoughts about choice or meaning in liberation?

There can be. When liberation is seen anything can still arise including thoughts about meaning or choice. But they're seen through. They can't be taken seriously because there's nobody there anymore to take them seriously.

I can't imagine what that could be like.

No, it's impossible. But when the sense of being a person drops away we may say "Oh my God! For forty years there was a sense of contraction." Until it drops away it doesn't feel like contraction, it just feels like the normal state.

Courage and the other qualities you listed are concepts. One of the things you might have heard said at a meeting about non-duality is there's no such thing as a relationship. That could sound quite scary to a person. But a relationship is a concept or a set of concepts. When there's no person there, when there's no relationship there, there may simply be a process of relating. That could feel a great deal deeper than having a relationship. It's similar to what I was saying about the mind. The mind is not an entity, it's a process, it's a flow of thoughts.

A relationship is an entity made out of concepts. Relating is a process. When the entity consisting of concepts has gone, it may be discovered that there is the possibility of deep intimacy in that process.

You've talked about unconditional love. How is it felt?

I wouldn't say it's felt. I can't get any closer than 'it's seen'. Words won't get any closer. The unconditionality of it is a real challenge, because 'unconditional' is tough. If you think of some of the things that go on in the story, it's pretty natural for the mind to say "How can that possibly be a manifestation of love?" Well, it is. And if it weren't, love wouldn't be unconditional. It would be conditional on certain things not happening. Love would embrace everything except that which we don't like.

When you say that the 'I' doesn't exist so I'm no longer here, you could also say that would mean the same thing as everyone is here. You said there's no such thing as the mind, but like the Buddhists you could say everything is mind. My own tradition is in Western spirituality so I'm quite comfortable with the idea that there is a common life, a common seeing. What you would describe as impersonal is a common seeing. Or is that a bit of a story?

It is. It's a story of all these interlocking universes.

But that wall is not interested in the story. It doesn't matter whether you know the wall is there or not. You could be looking in the other direction, not even thinking there's a wall there, but if you walk into it you'll bang your head. Anybody will, whether they're conscious of the wall or not. And that applies wherever there's a wall. So there seems to be something within the story that is common to everybody. There seems to be something solid in that sense.

Yes, there seems to be. But notice how that is in itself a story. All there is, is this. And part of what arises in this is a story that somehow there are commonalities and walls in other places and there are other places for walls to exist in. And there is time for walls to exist in. And that is all just a story. It might even be thought somewhere in this room that there was a talk that took place before a tea break and then tea was drunk. But no. This is it. There was no tea earlier and there will be no meal tonight. That's not a threat by the way – "If you ask any more awkward questions there will be no meal tonight!" *(Laughter)*

All right, there's no earlier. But I have a sensation of having eaten a huge piece of cake and I wouldn't have that if the piece of cake had not arisen, so there seems to be some continuity.

Yes, there certainly seems to be. There seems to be some continuity in watching a bird fly across the sky. Yet that continuity is only constructed in consciousness.

How do you cope, how do you manage practically, when you feel that there's no one there?

I don't feel that there's no one here. There's just no one here. And phenomena continue to arise. They might involve coping. Or getting angry on the phone with the electricity company.

Everything is completely impersonal?

Yes, completely impersonal. Then it appears that 'we' personalise it.

Would you ever get offended at something somebody said to you?

I would never get offended. But offence might arise. That thought or that feeling could definitely arise.

Is that not the ego?

What is the ego? This word 'ego' is a very difficult word because it can mean different things. We can get hooked very easily into another belief that somehow I have to get rid of my ego. It's absurd. If it's ego, it's ego. So what? Ego can still arise but for no one. Taking offence can arise. Getting angry with the electricity company can arise. Anything can arise, any phenomena.

So you can still take things personally?

I can't. But things can still be taken personally. Remember what I said earlier – there are no necessary implications and there are no rewards for a person in seeing liberation. But there may be a tendency for certain things to fall away or be less likely to arise. Taking offence may have something to do with the neurotic self. It's often a neurotic reaction. When the person leaves the premises it's possible that it might take some suitcases of neurosis with it. What might be left may be an emptier house. With less neurosis, the character that remains may not take offence so much. But it won't be impossible.

I was interested in whether you could say more about the sense of localisation.

Is there a sense of localisation there?

I don't know.

Localisation is simply the sense that there is a centre of awareness over here rather than over there. Phenomena arise and they seem to be arising in a particular place which appears to be separate from any other place.

I don't understand why that should still be there.

Neither do I. It's a mystery. Perhaps it's to do with the protection of the body-mind organism.

So there's still that sense of localisation?

Yes. But the sense of contraction that belongs to the person has gone. When you listen to others describing these events, this seems to be common. I can't throw any more light on it. I'm just trying to offer a description of something.

I can't imagine it.

No, that's the point. *You* can't.

Why not?

Because the sense of localisation and contraction have been with the person since the first moment of self-consciousness. In one way that's what self-consciousness consists of. It's a contraction into "I am here and I am in this and everything else is outside of me." If that is what has been experienced for forty years there can be no possibility of knowing what it is like when it is gone. So this can't be understood until that sense of contraction dissipates. Don't forget, we are talking about an energy shift here, not an idea or a belief. This energy shift consists in a sense of that contracted energy going 'bang'.

I don't understand that.

No, you can't.

Is it possible to have an experience where the physical sense doesn't come back?

In the sense of the total disappearance of localisation, that doesn't seem to happen permanently. This is, by the way, completely unimportant. We're just talking about phenomena here.

But it's beautiful. It's lovely to hear.

So are you disappointed to hear that this is it?

It's like you painted this lovely picture and then you took it away.

That may be because for a person the sense of localisation and the sense of contraction sound like they go together. If I say that localisation and contraction disappear and then I say that localisation returns, it may sound like that must mean contraction returns as well. But it doesn't. That's the difference.

I don't see how everything that's going on can be unconditional love.

All I can say is that it doesn't make sense until it makes sense. Then it's incontrovertible. But until then we may think it's nonsense. The mind may say "What are you talking about! Everything's unconditional love? What sort of world do you live in! Have you never poked your head outside the door and seen what's going on in the world! How can that be unconditional love?" There is no answer to that question other than the totally unsatisfactory one that when it's seen, it's seen. Remember that I've already said that the mind can't understand this. And understanding this with the mind isn't it in any case. So the mind looks at the world and is baffled by the statement that there's only unconditional love. The mind sees suffering and conflict in the world. Well, all I can do is offer a description which, as I said before, is bound to fail.

✳✳✳✳✳✳✳✳✳✳

You sound to me like someone talking about a religion – the Bible is true, the Koran is true and it is true because it is. I can't see much distinction between what you're saying and any religion.

I'll tell you the distinction. What you may think is sitting here is a fundamentalist non-dualist who is prepared to wage jihad on all those who disagree. *(Laughing)* The difference is I don't give a damn. It's as simple as that. There is no agenda here because there's no one here who feels there is any importance to anybody getting this.

Why do you come here?

It's just what's happening. Apparently there was a getting on a train at Kings Cross.

Did the train book itself?

Apparently there was the booking of the train. Apparently there was an invitation to come here way back last September and I said "I'll come up North but not till after the winter's over."
    There is no agenda here. There's nobody here who gives a damn about whether anybody gets this, not that anybody ever could get it. That's the difference between this and jihad. However, you probably know the saying from the Bible, "When two or three are gathered together in my name there shall be discord,

disharmony and a punch-up." I have confidently predicted that within ten years the world of non-duality will schism into several warring factions. I hope to be the leader of one of them and have a very big and important hat. *(Laughter)*

That's the difference and it's a pretty big difference. The point about most of the religious stories – not all of them – is that there is somebody who cares, who thinks that it matters that you should believe the same as they do. It doesn't matter. It's meaningless.

But we still have to take this on faith until it's seen.

Firstly, you don't have to take it on faith. Secondly, you can't take it on faith. What happens there in response to what is said here are just phenomena. They have nothing to do with you.

But I suspect that if people like yourself weren't making these statements then very few of us would be here. We're here in the hope that what you're saying is true.

That's just what it is like to be a person who is searching. All people are searching in some way or other. They might be searching for a more expensive Rolex watch but they're all searching.

You're here talking about this to us but you're saying that nothing matters. That seems like a contradiction.

It's just what's being drawn out of me by people trying to get me to say that something does matter.

My way of putting this is that everything is sacred

I like that way of putting it. I like the word 'sacred'. But I also feel that it can lead us into another set of stories. I might put it into more neutral language and perhaps deliberately so.

The reason that people are searching and the reason that there are all these stories is that for a person this isn't enough. When liberation is seen, it's seen that this is enough. It's a miracle. If you want to use the word 'sacred' for that, seeing everything as sacred, I think that's beautiful. I just tend to avoid that kind of language myself.

10

The Guru With
The Best Siddhis

When the mind hears statements like "There is no one" and "There is nothing happening", it is quite entitled to pipe up and say "Well, in that case, what's all the palaver about? There are people rushing about and wars and relationships and economic crises. There seems to be an awful lot going on for nothing to be happening."

The simplest way of answering this is "That's all stuff happening in the appearance. There is no one and stuff happens. Stuff looks like a lot of palaver. Sometimes it looks like people doing important and meaningful things."

To this, the mind might say "That's not a very satisfactory answer." In a way, the mind is right. As long as there is the sense of a separate person with a mind who acts in the world and has volition and makes free and significant choices, it doesn't make much sense to say that it's just stuff happening in the appearance. Where there's the sense of an individual, some of the stuff seems very important and some of it seems quite trivial. There are wars going on and there are cups of tea going on. Cups of tea seem pretty trivial compared to wars.

So another way of trying to explain this to the mind is to use the metaphor that Oneness is playing a game of hide and seek. But it's really difficult for Oneness to play hide and seek because it is already everything, so there's nowhere for it to hide. How can it hide as a person in the dark stairwell which leads to the cellar when it is the person, the stairwell and the cellar?

For this game of hide and seek to work, something else has to happen. Oneness not only needs to hide itself but it has to forget that it has done so. In order for it to hide successfully as people, the people have to forget that they are Oneness. People are simply Oneness, they are awareness being people. But they have to forget that this is what they are or there cannot be any search. If Oneness did not forget what it was, there would be nothing happening. There would be no palaver. There would be no wars, relationships, economic crises and cups of tea. We could say that Oneness has to forget where it has left itself, rather as we sometimes forget where we have left our keys.

So here we are, people rushing around looking for something but not really having the slightest idea of what it is because we've forgotten. We've forgotten the primal awareness of everything into which we were born. The primal awareness is not my awareness as an individual feeling at one with everything. It's seeing that I am everything and everything is one.

Almost none of us appear to be looking for Oneness directly because it's been forgotten so successfully. Although we know we've lost something, we don't know what it really is and so we appear to be searching for something else – a lot of money, a relationship, an opportunity to slaughter the heathens, the founding of a charity or the saving of the planet, opportunities to do good or harm in innumerable ways.

We could make a very long list of all the things that we're searching for because we can't remember what it is we've actually lost. It's worse than losing our keys. Firstly we've forgotten where we've left our keys, but secondly we've forgotten that it's our keys we're looking for. So it is a double mystery. "Where is it and what is it? Is it God? Is it a big house in the country? Is it the perfect romantic relationship? What is it that will fill this sense of lack?" We are continually looking for substitutes for the sense of Oneness because we have so thoroughly forgotten that Oneness is what we want to find. This is what fuels the sometimes desperate activity that seems to be going on.

There is a wonderful balance to this activity. There might be a number of people who are searching for death from alcoholism. That's a surprisingly common goal. But there will also be a number of people searching to save alcoholics from themselves by setting up a hostel for alcoholics. There will always be that balance.

We might try romance, gambling, warfare and alcoholism in that order. Or shopping, then religion. Often we think that we have found what we're searching for, and then the suspicion begins to grow that this isn't what it's about after all because we still feel that there's something missing. So some of us begin to think that none of these things are it. It's not a big house, it's not God, it's not saving the planet. That might be when some of us start looking for Oneness directly and end up at a talk like this.

There are a few people for whom the game of hide and seek doesn't quite work. For them, Oneness has hidden but it hasn't quite been forgotten. These people tend to look for Oneness directly without bothering about the allure of relationships, Rolex watches, slaughtering heathens or saving the planet. There are even rare cases of those who never lost Oneness in the first place and never really had the solid sense of being a separate individual. If you read accounts of Krishnamurti's early life, it's possible that for him there wasn't the sense of being a person in the way that most of us know it. That was probably what attracted the Theosophists to him. Later on he said "Truth is a pathless land." That's a pretty good hint that practices, beliefs and concepts are of no use here. I prefer "Truth is a pathless land" to an invitation to touch the guru's feet any day.

But we cannot bear to be told that as 'I' am not a person, there is nothing that I can do about finding Oneness. We are so used to taking action to reach a goal. If there's a hole in my roof, I can repair it. If I need to pass an exam, I can work for it. But finding Oneness is the one thing that we cannot do anything about.

What do you think of Sathya Sai Baba?

For some of us who are attracted to spiritual paths, if we have a certain kind of personality, we may be attracted most powerfully to figures who seem to be able to do magic, who seem to have siddhis or yogic powers. Many spiritual seekers, often the more ascetically inclined, would not go near anything like that but some are very drawn to it. They adore the thought of magic and siddhis.

If we make a connection between spiritual power and siddhis, we're likely to want to go to whoever seems best at doing magic, to whoever seems to have the most siddhis. You can account for Sai Baba's popularity in this way.

We might first think there's a connection between happiness and 'spiritual growth'. We might then think that 'spiritual growth' is evidenced by 'magical powers'. If we make that equation, we might go to see someone like Sai Baba.

Anyone who offers 'salvation' of any kind in any way can seem very attractive if our personality is hooked in by it. If our main interest is gambling, we might be hooked in by a guru of the race track who can offer us salvation through a good tip. If the priest offers us eternal life and that's our form of salvation, it's very difficult to turn it down. If our form of salvation is 'spiritual progress delineated by the acquiring of siddhis' and somebody seems to be offering that, it's very difficult to say no.

Some people are attracted by siddhis and some people are repulsed by them. When Maharishi began to offer his siddhi programme within the Transcendental Meditation movement, many people signed up for it but many other people, including some of his teachers, left his organisation.

We could say it's just an aspect of the flavour of the personality. One personality is attracted to developing siddhis, another personality is repulsed by them and a third personality is attracted to the pub or the betting shop to try to find a guru of the race track. None of this makes the finding of Oneness any more or any less likely.

Is there any real difference between traditional stories about God in the sky and this new story of non-duality? Is this story as meaningless as any other story?

Yes, it is as meaningless. But it's not new. The seeing that there is no person keeps spontaneously happening without any cause. Sometimes when it's seen, an energy arises to communicate about it.

It's not new, but it might seem new. When it's communicated, the listeners tend to mishear it, misunderstand it, misconstrue it, mistranslate it, pass it on to others in a mistaken form and then turn it into a religion.

This is what the Buddha saw. Look at what's happened since to the communication he made about it. Now we not only have Buddhism, we have about a hundred forms of Buddhism. We have Pure Land Buddhism, Nichiren Shoshu Buddhism, Vajrayana Buddhism and many others. But you can't blame that on the Buddha. He did his best to communicate that which he knew could not be communicated

Although never a Buddhist, I have some fondness for Buddhism. If we're going to have a religion, we might as well have a sensible one. In the story of history, the early Christians were very like the Taliban are today. If they had reached the Indian subcontinent, they would have wiped out Buddhism. They wiped out Paganism, slaughtered the priests, burnt the books, destroyed the temples. They'd have done the same to Buddhism.

But in a sense, that wouldn't have mattered because what the Buddha saw just keeps on being seen. It keeps spontaneously arising.

So does it matter which spiritual or religious story we listen to or don't listen to?

No. It's completely meaningless. It has no importance whatsoever. Nevertheless, this story points as directly as possible to Oneness whereas most stories point directly away from it. And there are some stories that point towards this in an indirect way. But none of that matters at all. It's no better and no worse to talk about God in the sky than it is to talk about this. It's just that some of us are attracted to this story and some of us to different stories. There are different personalities with different flavours.

Of course in the world of phenomena where stuff happens, some of these stories tend to lead to a lot of slaughter, while others don't. This story doesn't tend to lead to slaughter. There hasn't been a Non-duality Crusade yet. But if more and more people become interested in the story of Non-duality, there may well be one. There may be a huge schism and eventually a Non-duality war.

But it's implicit in this story that there is a greater liking for liberation than in other stories.

Yes, but the mind which thinks that it has a liking for liberation can't possibly understand what liberation is. The mind may be attracted to it but it can't understand what that attraction is. However it suspects that in some way liberation must be 'a good thing', that liberation must be better than the absence of liberation. I'd be a bit wary of that. Remember the Zen saying: "Why do you want liberation? How do you know you'd like it?"

But as there's no choice about it, it doesn't really matter.

✸✸✸✸✸✸✸✸✸✸

I read on a non-duality website that we're slowly dying. It seemed an odd thing to say.

Well, we're all slowly dying biologically. Except for those of us who are dying quickly.

But the death of the separate person in the sense we talk about it here is not a process?

It's not a process. We can't do anything to bring it about. There's no cause and effect. However, in the story of time there may be awakening and later on liberation may be seen. Between what may seem to be these two events, the sense of being a separate individual may come and go. In the dream in which stuff happens, that could seem like a process. But there is no process because nothing is actually happening.

Asking questions about this seems hopeless.

Some people ask a lot of questions at first but then stop. At first the mind can be very puzzled and often very angry about this. It will look for a hook that it can grab onto. The mind may think "If I pay enough attention, if I ask the right question, there will be a hook that I can use to haul myself up the cliff face of enlightenment." Later on that can gradually die away because the mind begins to see that it is not going to get anywhere. As soon as it grabs onto a hook, the hook just falls out of the cliff. So the mind gives up. It may give up asking questions, give up listening, even give up staying awake. *(Laughing)* Of course sleeping through these talks is a sign of being very spiritually evolved.

I get to the point of thinking "Sod it."

That may be a sign of the mind giving up. I'm not saying that's helpful, but it can be more relaxing to be here in a half-awake haze rather than in a state of furious agitation.

Different people communicate this message in very different ways.

If the communication is clear, that's just the flavour of the personality. Some personalities like talking about different stories within the story. I like doing that. Others won't talk about stories at all.

But often there is a communication which claims to be about non-duality but is completely misleading. This will usually be a version in some form or other of "I can teach you how to do 'being'. If you sit here close enough to me for long enough you can catch 'being' from me like the small-pox." This is a very common communication from gurus. With luck, although you won't catch enlightenment, you won't catch small-pox either.

If we want to be misled, we'll go to communicators who will mislead us. If we want to be told that there is something that we can do in order to move ourself closer to enlightenment, through tantric yoga for example, we'll go to someone who is teaching that. We'll avoid communications which are just a clear simple description of this. They won't be exciting enough for us. But they'll attract the people who want that simplicity.

This is no more mysterious than someone who is interested in opera going to the Royal Opera House rather than to a cricket match. The fact that you are sitting here suggests that you are more interested in hearing about Oneness than in trying to catch enlightenment from a guru.

It's very difficult to talk about this without suggesting either that there's nothing going on here apart from the words, or that being here for long enough and paying enough money will make the person drop away. Both of these are misleading. This is something else for the mind to bang its head against in frustration. The mind lives in duality and duality often gives us the choice between black and white. So the mind says "Come on! Tell me! Is being here going to do me some good or not? It must be one or the other." The answer to that, which the mind doesn't like, is neither.

Actually it doesn't matter whether being here is a waste of time, or will guarantee the dropping of the self, because there's no choice about being here and there is nobody who is here. The understanding of this can cut through the question and render it irrelevant. There's no person, no choice, and what's happening is just what's happening.

11
A Very Simple Secret

I recently read an article about Ken Wilbur by John Heron. It was highly critical but what struck me most is that Ken Wilbur's Integral Psychology, his view of how we and the cosmos are, is incredibly complex and seems to develop ever more complexity. But it is understandable. You can comprehend it with the mind if you study it, although you may find contradictions in it.

It's the exact opposite of what we are here to talk about this afternoon. Non-Duality is incredibly simple but it is incomprehensible to the mind. It doesn't matter how much the mind studies this, it will never get it. We can study this and understand concepts about it, but the mind will never approach what non-duality actually is.

The mind could analyse and fully understand the constituents of an orange but that wouldn't give us any idea of what one tastes like. But once we've tasted one, its flavour is incontrovertible whether we understand what constituents it contains or not. In the same way, we can have a very good understanding of non-duality but that won't tell us what liberation tastes like.

The Transcendental Meditation movement offers a course called the Science of Creative Intelligence. This course is also very complex, though not as complex as Ken Wilbur's psycho-philosophy. Maharishi designed this course after he decided that it was bad PR to talk about God in the West, so he started talking about science and quantum physics instead.

For me, after searching for about three decades, the suspicion began to grow that if there was a secret, it had to be very simple. I had a feeling that there was a secret, that there was something about life or reality or existence that I wasn't getting, but there was no real certainty about this. So I was putting a great deal of energy into looking for this secret without being absolutely sure that it even existed, but feeling that if it did exist, it was very simple. Before even meeting non-duality there was a turning away from all the complex stories, like Tibetan Buddhism with its multiple worlds and its many levels of being.

When liberation is seen it is utterly simple. But it is also astonishing. And it is obvious in a way that can't be explained. It becomes clear in a split second why all the things that the mind ever did, all the stories it became fascinated by, all the techniques it practised, all the revolutions of the mantra it repeated, could never possibly have got anyone anywhere. The revelation is that none of this could have got anyone anywhere because there isn't anyone. The secret is and always has been that there is no one. There is simply emptiness at the core. That's actually only half the story but we'll come back to that later.

Tony Parsons' first book was called 'The Open Secret'. It's not as if the secret is hidden under a rock. There was never any necessity to search for it and there was never any possibility that a person could find it. I'm sorry if this is a tautology, but when it becomes obvious, it's obvious. It's even too distant to say that it's staring us in the face. It isn't staring us in the face because there's no it, there's no us and there's no face. "It's staring us in the face" is clearly a dualistic statement. 'It' is out there, and I'm over here with a face and somehow I can bring 'it' and 'me' together, 'I' can get closer to 'it'.

This is what the spiritual paths are about, getting closer to it. That's what I had been doing in the story of time for thirty years. I had been making very serious and at times apparently quite successful attempts to get closer to it. It felt at times as though it could almost be tasted and almost be seen and yet it was still hidden.

When the obvious reveals itself and the open secret isn't a secret anymore, none of this applies. It's not staring us in the face because there aren't these two things, us and it, one of which can get closer to the other through religions or spiritual paths or self-enquiry or through suppressing the mind or through Being Here Now. None of this is relevant because the whole idea that I can get near to the secret is a misconception. But it's such a profound misconception that the mind can't see through it, no matter what it does. It can't fail to misunderstand it. It's the very existence of the mind going "Jabber, jabber, jabber, there is somewhere for you to get to and I can get you to it" that prevents the seeing of the obvious. The mind says "I can get you there. Meditate. Self-enquire. Kiss the guru's feet. Keep a relic of the guru's toenail clippings like the blackened, wizened fingers of saints found in silver reliquaries in Italian churches." The mind says "There is a journey that can be taken to somewhere that's better than this." In a sense that's what fuels the drama of life, this feeling that there is somewhere better than this. The adage "The grass is greener on the other side of the valley" drives us through life. We think "This isn't it. There must be somewhere better than this, where I will feel whole and harmonious and satisfied."

So the mind takes us on a journey. For many of us sitting here it may be a spiritual or a philosophical journey. For other people it may be the journey of shopping or the journey of gambling or the journey of becoming an alcoholic. It's all the same thing in a sense.

It isn't meant to be frivolous if I draw an equivalence between "I'll feel better when I've meditated" and "I'll feel better when I'm drunk", between thirty years spent meditating, thirty years spent as an alcoholic, thirty years spent in a betting shop or thirty years spent in the Catholic Church. The mind might revolt against this and say "That is absolutely ridiculous. Thirty years spent in a betting shop is a waste of time but thirty years spent meditating is highly meaningful." But there will be somebody else saying exactly the opposite. At the race track there will be somebody saying "Thirty years of meditation is a complete waste of time but thirty years of gambling is the ultimate in fulfilment."

So I'm not being frivolous in drawing an equivalence between these different stories. And I'm not ignoring the fact that in the play, in the story of a person's life, they do have different effects. I don't recommend alcoholism as a way of making ourselves more comfortable. I'd recommend meditation for that. So you might say "Well, you're not really drawing an equivalence, are you." I'm drawing an equivalence in meaning. I'm not drawing an equivalence in terms of outcomes in the daily life of a person, the stuff that happens. Meditation doesn't lead to cirrhosis of the liver. But in terms of meaning and purpose and the reaching of some desired goal that's seen as being somewhere else that's better than this in a future time, I'm drawing an equivalence. It doesn't matter whether we meditate, go shopping, become an alcoholic, study philosophy or do therapy and develop ourselves. In terms of meaning and purpose it makes no difference though it will make a difference to the story. In the same way, if we buy a ticket to 'Hamlet' we will have a different sort of evening than if we buy a ticket to 'Rigoletto' or to 'Arsenal'. But in terms of there being somewhere purposeful to get to or a meaningful goal to be achieved, it makes no difference whether we're meditating or standing on an escalator in a department store.

For the mind this is one of the most frustrating things about this. The mind might say "That is really unfair. I've spent thousands of pounds on meditation courses, I've had months of agony eating rice and catching hideous diseases sitting in an ashram in the Himalayas, and some guy may be out shopping and suddenly there's no one shopping, there's just the seeing that there is no one."

It is as simple as that. If there's a recognition of what I'm saying, then it's obvious, but if there isn't, the mind can't get this. That's all we're talking about here. There may be someone shopping, and then there may be no one shopping but nevertheless shopping is still going on and it is seen that there is no one. In terms of awakening, that might only last half a second, but it's revelatory. It's a revelation to discover that shopping can go on without any need of a person to shop.

This is the nothing that's talked about here. There's a strong tendency to connect this with the philosophy of Advaita. It is in Advaita that this is expressed in the most complex and elegant way for the philosophical mind. The word 'non-duality' is after all the nearest English equivalent to 'advaita'. But really this has no more connection to Advaita than to anything else. The seeing that here there is nothing, that there is no one, can occur spontaneously in any culture, at any time and in any tradition.

One of the reasons that the ideas around this became developed more highly within Advaita was that in Indian culture, if you talked about this, you weren't taken outside and executed by the Inquisition. But within Christianity, people who saw this and talked about it or wrote about it tended to have very short lives. Very quickly they could be on trial for heresy and soon after that they might be burning on a pyre. So it's not surprising that within Advaita this became developed in a more complex way. Nevertheless, if you look at certain Christian mystics and at Buddhism and at Sufism, for example, as well as at Advaita, it is quite clear that the seeing of this keeps occurring in different cultures. And it keeps being misunderstood.

It keeps being talked about because it keeps being seen. No matter what the culture or the religion or the philosophical background, over and over again there is somebody and then suddenly there is nobody. This is a repeated happening throughout the story of human history, pretending for the moment that there is such a thing.

Then there may be an attempt to communicate about it. Some of these attempts are clearer than others.

This seeing that there is no one is an uncaused spontaneous happening which has no relation to anything else. It is not caused by thirty years of meditation or by paying subscriptions to a spiritual society. But after the person has disappeared they often come back and make up very misleading stories about how they

211

themselves produced this event. Their story will often be based on what they had been doing prior to disappearing. If they had been meditating, for example, they might now set up a School of Enlightenment Through Meditation and start teaching confusion about this.

Even when there is a clear communication about liberation, the mind of the listener will often get hold of it and misunderstand and misinterpret it. The mind has a strong tendency to translate this into something that it thinks it can understand. It will usually come up with some version or other of the same idea – that the mind itself can get the person to realise liberation by doing something, by practising some technique or by following some path.

My mind seems to understand the concept of being there and not being there.

In a sense that's the point I'm trying to make. The mind can understand this intellectually but that's like knowing what the constituents of an orange are but not knowing its taste.

When I go shopping, it's for a reason. It's because I have a need.

Yes, there seems to be cause and effect.

Need seems to be related to some condition.

You might want to make a cup of tea so you buy a kettle.

So if I always have needs related to my conditioning, how can the absence of me ever be experienced?

That's what the mind says. "How can a kettle be bought when there's no one buying it?" Of course the mind says that this doesn't make sense. But when the secret is seen, it's both a revelation and very obvious. That's why there might be an exclamation of "Of course! Of course that's what it is!"

As a person, I am likely to think throughout my life that the secret is either about something out there in the world or something inside me. Either my life will work when I've got enough money to buy a Mercedes, or my life will work when I've cleared all my chakric blocks. All forms of searching, all forms of belief that I can make this o.k. for myself in some future time, relate to out there or to inside me. Of course buying a Mercedes is a metaphor for all the stuff out there and clearing my chakric blocks is a metaphor for all the different kinds of work that I can do on myself. It seems clear to us that making our life work has got to be about one of those because that's all there is. Either I'll be happy when I've adjusted the stuff out there sufficiently or I'll be happy when I've adjusted the stuff inside me sufficiently. How can the mind possibly see through that?

So of course it's a revelation when both of these are seen to be irrelevant. The secret has got nothing to do with 'out there' and it's got nothing to do with 'inside me'. Instead it has to do with seeing that there is no 'out there' and there is no 'inside me'. There is only nothing in which the appearance of everything arises, emptiness giving rise to all phenomena. The Christian mystics sometimes called this the abyss. It is the void out of which all phenomena arise.

That doesn't sound very attractive, does it? If 'the void' sounds bleak and nihilistic, remember that when nothing is fully seen, it is seen to be full. This is a paradox which the mind can't make any sense of. It sounds like nonsense to the mind. But when the abyss is fully seen, it's seen to contain a full emptiness. Out of this emptiness all phenomena arise, including the sense that I am a separate person, that there's an individual here who got on a train this morning and travelled here today. For that to be seen to be empty is astonishing.

Nobody got on a train and travelled here today. More depressingly, nobody will have tea at half-past three.

When it's said that "Nothing is happening" does that mean that No Thing is happening or does it mean that nothing is happening?

Both. There is an appearance in which it looks like something is happening. It would be more accurate to say that No Thing is happening, No Thing is giving rise to an apparent series of events. No Thing is giving rise to the appearance of time. That's important because stuff can only happen in time.

But actually, there's no time and there's nothing happening. If you recall what you were apparently doing last night, it has the quality of a dream. It is no different in quality to something you are imagining. But that won't satisfy the mind. The mind will say "Excuse me! I had dinner last night! There are washed-up plates on the draining board to prove it!" All I can reply is that what is being said here is a description. When liberation is seen, time is seen through.

So "Nothing is happening" means there are no events?

Yes. That's an accurate description.

And there are no people? There's no one here and there's no one there? Yet you refer to us as though we exist.

That's the nature of language. I've referred to numerous things this afternoon that don't exist; cups of tea, the mind, the train that I came here on and the 'me' that came here.

We could avoid talking about any of that. Everything we've talked about this afternoon is a story, including getting on trains and travelling to London. There are people who communicate about this who don't talk about such aspects of the story, but I do. It must be obvious that I enjoy talking about the story.

****

In a certain sense what you're saying is blindingly obvious.

It can be blindingly obvious to the mind as concepts, or it can be seen in which case it's incontrovertible.

214

It flip-flops here. It's blindingly obvious when you're talking about it and when attention is paid to it. But when I'm driving down the motorway planning my next job, that all takes place in apparent time and there's an apparent person doing it and there's a real sense of someone being there.

There's a going in and out of being a person. That's very common.

Is there some kind of event whereby this flip-flopping ceases?

There are no rules about this. Here there were two events. In the first, emptiness was seen and the existence of the person was seen through, but then the person came back and was still searching. In the second event there was a different kind of seeing, because emptiness was seen also to be full. After that the person didn't come back. But it doesn't matter. There can be a gliding into this. There doesn't have to be any event that's recognised. There's nothing we can do about it anyway, but if there is an event perhaps it makes it easier to talk about this because it can put a punctuation mark, a full-stop, to the existence of the person.

The pursuit of an event is just another story?

Yes, the pursuit of an event, which can fuel spiritual seeking, is just another story. But as long as there's the mind of a person there, that can't really be seen. I can argue myself into thinking "Of course the sense of self is false and so it's ridiculous for a false self to look for reality" or "How could a false self ever see real love?" I can argue my mind into agreeing with this but it doesn't have anything to do with seeing what we're talking about. Nothing that the mind can think, nothing that the mind can argue, nothing that the mind has to say, has anything to do with this.

Is the mind trying to find some kind of permanence in what you've just described, in the sense that it's gliding in and out but wanting

215

to be in this all the time? Am I right in saying the mind is wanting to capture this, this sense of non-personal being?

Yes, in the experience of a person, the one who feels themself to be an individual, that's a good way of putting it. The person's sense is that the mind wants to find completion and fulfilment. The mind believes that this isn't it but there is something else that is it. So the mind looks for something satisfying somewhere else. But of course there isn't really any mind which is doing that. More accurately, we could say that Oneness is pretending that it isn't Oneness in order to look for itself. Nothing is looking for itself.

In daily life is it inevitable that we have to go in and out?

As a description, that will do. Although there is no us and there is no going in and out, for a person it's likely to be seen like that. This seems to be what happens for people. We may be 'on automatic' cooking rice and in a sense we are not there. Then something may come into our mind and we're back. We might think "Oh God, I'm depressed today. I wonder whether I'd feel better if I went on that meditation retreat."

Or somebody might communicate with us or a neighbour might pop in?

We could say that sometimes the person comes back more strongly. Often that happens when there's a lot of suffering. There are few things like suffering for making the person feel really solid. And sometimes the person might come back but in a rather evanescent way.

Are you saying this occurs for Richard?

It doesn't occur for Richard and it doesn't occur for you. It doesn't occur for anybody. If the question is "What is the daily experience for Richard?" the important thing to say is that phenomena don't necessarily change. "Before liberation, hewing wood. After liberation, hewing wood." Having said that, there are tendencies for certain kinds of phenomena to lessen or drop away. For example, there's a tendency for neurotic phenomena to drop away but there's no necessity for this to happen. Neuroses belong to the person, so when the person leaves they may take their neuroses with them. But they may not. The person may leave the house and take their suitcases of neuroses with them or they may leave slamming the door behind them and the suitcases of neuroses are still lying around in the hall.

As far as Richard's experience is concerned there's no in and out?

There's no in and out because there's no 'Richard's experience.' But there's no in and out for you either. Nevertheless in the appearance of time phenomena may happen which are associated with in and out; in the person, out of the person. Here that's seen through.

That's a common perception. One understands this and then one gets carried away with the story.

Understanding is just a thought. Thought is constantly changing. No thought hangs around for long. It might be a wonderful thought about existential philosophy but fifteen seconds later it might be "I need a pee now". Whether liberation is seen or not, thought is constantly changing. Actually everything is constantly changing but it's particularly noticeable that thought is. But while there's a person, there's a sensation that the person is giving rise to the thoughts. And much more uncomfortably perhaps, that the person can control those thoughts. Even more uncomfortably, that the person can stop thoughts arising by 'Being Here Now'.

There always seems to be some new need arising.

There's always the next thing happening, apparently. If we become interested in spiritual paths, the idea that there must be a state of permanent bliss which can be achieved has an extraordinary grip on the mind. That must be the solution to the feelings of dissatisfaction, vulnerability and inadequacy of being a person. It's amazing that we think this, because from the first moment that we become self-conscious everything is shouting at us that the one thing we can be absolutely sure of is that there is no permanence. Everything is clearly in a constant state of flux.

Yet this idea has such a grip on us and holds such magical promise for us that in spite of the evidence of our whole lifetime, the belief that there must be a permanent state of bliss often survives.

Which is a misconception?

Yes, it's a misconception. It's an extraordinarily powerful idea that retains a hold over us in spite of the fact that every phenomenon that we come across contradicts it. Every phenomenon that we come across is there and then it's not there.

Are you saying that everything is relative, everything is conditioned? If something happens, then it causes something else to happen?

No, because there's nothing happening. But it looks like there is. I'm saying that in the world of the appearance where it seems that things are happening, everything that appears to be happening is evanescent, time-bound, changeable, changing. Impermanent, as the Buddhists call it.

****

What is the value of the absolute?

What is its value? It has no value. It doesn't need to have a value. What is the value of an oak tree? It doesn't need to have a value, it just is.

Some say the absolute exists as the opposite of the relative.

That's an idea that has gripped some of the philosophical minds in the Indian tradition for centuries. It's a very attractive idea. It sets the mind racing like a hare sets greyhounds racing. The mind needs a hare to chase, otherwise it gets bored. It needs an idea which will set it running round an evolutionary or developmental race-track. The idea that there is the absolute and the relative and somehow I can bring them together or harmonise them is fascinating because it can produce infinite philosophical complexity about how I might be able to do that. In a sense that's where all the yogas spring from.

What the mind needs in order to keep its search going is two opposing ideas. Religions and spiritual paths and philosophies are usually not just dualistic, they deal in binary opposites. They deal in good and evil, moral and immoral, that which will take us to heavenly bliss and that which will take us to eternal torment. Religions usually walk through history on the two legs of intimidation and seduction. "If you don't obey us you will suffer eternal torture but if you do obey us you will have eternal bliss. Eventually, after you've died, so you can't sue us."

That's what I mean by binary opposites. It's not just dualistic. A leaf falling from a tree is a dualistic phenomenon. But the mind has a tendency to set up these binary opposites. That's what it loves, that's what the mind finds most juicy. Once the mind has set up good and evil, heaven and hell, intimidation and seduction, it's up and running. These are the hares that will have it racing round the track. Everything that we now do becomes meaningful and purposeful, down to whether we say our prayers before we go to bed or put a donation in the collection box or have an angry thought or a charitable thought about our neighbour. God is now keeping his eye on us, noting down the minutiae of our every word, thought and deed in the profit and loss account of our life.

If we set up an opposition between God and Satan, heaven and hell, good and evil, then everything becomes imbued with meaning. At an extreme, the opportunity to dance on a Sunday may be sent by Satan to tempt us away from our ascetic path to our doom. Our righteousness might be compromised by a Sabbath polka.

One of the things the person most wants is meaning. It can be very distressing if meaning drops away but the person is still there. That often leads to depression. It's one of the curses of existentialism. We may get involved with existentialism and two years later the person may still be solidly there but meaning may have dropped away. We may have seen through meaning, seen that all the stories are nonsense. That can often lead to a state of depression.

If the person drops away it takes meaning with them. But if meaning drops away it can leave the person behind, possibly feeling very sorry for themself.

You need meaning to be happy.

If there's a person there, it's a good idea to attach our life to a meaning if we want to be happy. If the person drops away, it will take that meaning with it. But that's o.k. It might leave laughter and walking round the park instead.

For a person to live a happy life, it's obvious that some things work better than others. Being nice to people sometimes works quite well. So does having a project.

Religious people have a tendency to be really nice.

That sometimes arises from a different impulse. They sometimes rigorously suppress their shadow. Here we have another fundamental pair of binary opposites. Many of us have outgrown the religious opposites like God and Satan. Instead, we may recognise the opposites of persona and shadow. Our persona is the part of ourself which we feel it is acceptable to express to other people because we accept it in ourself. Our shadow is the part of ourself which we hide from other people because we reject it in ourself. From a psychological perspective we could suggest that this is where the metaphysical opposites stem from. God and Satan can be seen as projections of our persona and shadow.

Once we have devoted ourself to God and rejected Satan, there are likely to be numerous impulses that we feel we have to push into the shadow. In psychological terms this means that many religious people have very large shadows. This explains why they are sometimes rather dangerous and inclined to kill one another. That's what tends to happen when the shadow is suppressed, we project it onto others and see them as evil. If it's not dealt with, the shadow can emerge in very destructive ways. Jung said that when we fail to deal with our shadow, not only do we burn down our own house but the flames leap out and set fire to our neighbour's house as well. This happens literally. A group of people project all that is 'evil' onto another group and attack them. The second group retaliate and everybody's house is burned down.

It has been said that there will always be good people who do good things and bad people who do bad things, but to get good people to do bad things you need religion.

If you attach your life to a meaning and you suddenly disappear, it doesn't necessarily mean that you drop the goals you've had in your life.

It does necessarily mean that *you* don't have those goals anymore because you're not there, but those goals could still manifest. So there may be no change to goals. Remember that the seeing of liberation is completely impersonal. It doesn't have anything to do with anyone, not with this character or with that character.

As soon as we start expecting to find certain necessary characteristics in the individual who is talking about liberation, we're off on another mistaken path of the mind. We may think "If liberation is seen, surely the individual must have risen above wanting to own a house in the country or to have affairs with blonde starlets or to drink lots of whisky." This is just another set of mental concepts. "Liberation must have something to do with whatever I consider purity to be."

As I've said before, gurus sometimes get up to shenanigans. We may be quite surprised when a guru who's been teaching celibacy for thirty years and enforcing celibacy in their ashram is caught in the women's dormitory. Nevertheless that is completely irrelevant to what we're talking about here. This doesn't have anything to do with character, personality, behaviour or morality. "God knows no morality." This has nothing to do with whether there is a desire to visit the women's dormitory through a secret tunnel in the ashram, or to visit the stock of single malts through a different tunnel.

Paradoxically, the dropping of the ego seems to happen mostly where the person has had a powerful ego. This falling away of the ego seems to happen to those egos which are particularly strong.

It sounds like you're developing a method there. Strengthen your ego as much as you can and maybe it will fall away.

Perhaps it requires some kind of egoic strength to get rid of the ego.

This has nothing to do with a person getting rid of their ego. It has to do with the disappearance of the person, which is not the same thing.

Is the ego not that which claims ownership?

Whatever we mean by 'ego', it has nothing to do with the sense of self dropping away, because nothing has anything to do with that. There is no cause of that. But the ego, because it is connected to the personality, may have something to do with whether a communication is made about this or not after it's happened.

Neither you nor I know how many bus conductors or taxi drivers have been travelling down the road when the person has fallen away and perhaps they never talk about it to anyone because there isn't that kind of personality there.

Sometimes people say to me "Haven't you noticed that most of the people talking about this actually did meditate for a long time before 'it' happened?" My answer to that is still "There is no causation whatsoever." But it's possible that if there was the following of a spiritual path for some years previous to the seeing of liberation, perhaps there might be more of an impulse to communicate about it.

It's very difficult for the mind not to look for causation. The mind lives in the world of phenomena and that is a world of cause and effect.

You're saying that the impulse to own a house in the country can happen without a person?

I'm saying more than that. I'm saying that it is already happening without a person. There isn't anyone who wants to own a house in the country but there might be the thought "I am an individual and I want to do that."

Everything exists without there being a person. The desire to become the dictator of a small Latin American country in the mind of the Generalissimo is happening without a person.

Perhaps it's the mischief of my mind that wants to understand the mechanism behind the non-person.

The mind is not mischievous. Wanting to understand is what the mind does. It's what it has to do. If we listen to enough spiritual teachers, everything is condemned. One spiritual teacher says the mind is an impediment, another says the body and its desires are an impediment. One guru says the body is a disease, another says thinking is a disease. If we listen to enough gurus we end up as a mass of diseases.

So is the mind at fault?

The mind's function is to think. That's the same as saying "In Oneness, thought arises." It's not mischievous or at fault. It's just what the mind does. But in essence you're right, the mind will seek to understand.

But if the root of wanting to own a big house was the desire to feel a more powerful person in relationship to other people, and the sense of a person falls away, then the basis for wanting a big house would also fall away.

It might do. There are no necessary implications in this but there is a tendency for certain phenomena to diminish such as neurotic tendencies. And psychopathic ones. But they don't have to. Anything can happen.

If there was a character who had a desire to own a big house, the fact that the person drops away doesn't mean that the character changes. It doesn't change the goal that is inherent in that body-mind, which is just Oneness expressing itself anyway.

It may or it may not. There are no rules. Before the seeing of liberation, anything can happen. After the seeing of liberation, anything can happen. As I've said before, if you want phenomena to change, don't seek liberation, take hallucinogenic drugs. That will change phenomena astonishingly quickly and in many very colourful ways. But what I'm talking about here is not phenomena changing. It's simply seeing that there is no one for whom those phenomena are happening and that there is no one who is causing them to happen.

I've heard that if you're offered a million dollars or enlightenment, you should take the money because there'd be no one there to enjoy the enlightenment.

Perhaps it's fortunate that none of us are going to be put to that choice because you can't be offered enlightenment.

****

We love to be special and different. This can manifest in apparently opposite ways. Perhaps we'll be special and different by accumulating power and wealth or perhaps by making ourself a particularly humble servant of the Lord. If we're a spiritual seeker, we might find a teacher who is special and different. The more special the teacher is, the more special we become. If we've found not just a teacher but an avatar, that makes us extremely special. If they are the Avatar or the Maitreya or the Returning Christ, this shows that we are particularly spiritually discerning because we have been able to see the qualities of this great master.

But as I was saying earlier, liberation is totally impersonal. It has nothing to do with the qualities of a teacher or a guru or an avatar.

The mind connects liberation to several things erroneously. Liberation has nothing to do with feelings. It has nothing to do with feeling better. It has nothing to do with happiness. Happiness might arise or it might not arise. It has nothing to do with suffering or an end to suffering. Suffering might arise or it might not arise. In fact, it has nothing to do with anything that is subjectively experienced.

What instrument do you use when you think about seeing this experience in order to verify or validate it?

You can't verify or validate it and it's not an experience. Could you say what you mean by 'instrument'?

I mean which sense. In duality there are ways of finding out for yourself whether something's true or false. When this is seen through, it has to be done with something. If the mind is not the instrument, then what is?

There is no instrument. The revelation is that the person is gone and yet everything continues. Until that's seen, it's unimaginable because it is only possible to imagine things based on personal experience. But if you want a word, I usually use 'seeing'. This is just seen. Or we could say that the appearance is seen through. But I don't literally mean 'seen with the eyes'. That's just the closest word I can use. That seems better than saying it's tasted or it's felt or it's touched. But when the person isn't there, there is no instrument. There is just awareness. There is just Oneness being aware.

Whether there is the sense of a contracted person or not, there is usually a sense of location, a locus of awareness in a place that seems to exist separately from other places. But this is just an appearance. There is no actual locus of awareness. There is no awareness here in this character but not in those walls, for example. There is no separation at all in that sense. But how could that possibly be described? Of course the walls aren't aware, but awareness is just as much in the walls as here.

Awareness isn't located in the brain. There's no separation between the brain and the wall or between the brain and anything else.

The Hindu tradition of the different auric sheaths and the subtle bodies and the chattering mind and the discriminating mind doesn't seem to have a massive place in your description.

No, it doesn't have any place at all. But it's a very good story and it can be very convincing. One of the most powerful faculties of the mind is imagination. The mind is fantastically powerful at creating imaginary worlds and visions, both imaginary conceptual worlds and imaginary sensory worlds. Once we get into a story like that which might start with concepts about the chattering mind and the discriminating mind and the various auric sheaths and the subtle bodies, it can become extremely real. In the same way, if we get into the story of psychic channelling, dead Aunt Beatrice can become extremely real. The mind is very powerful in that sense.

Once we are inside a complex story, it is very difficult to get out of it. It becomes an all-encompassing bubble. It has been said that those who study the Kabala, for example, find it very difficult to break away from it.

But none of these stories have any bearing on liberation. This cuts through everything, through every story. It doesn't matter whether it's the wizened saint's finger in its reliquary in St Peter's or whether it's the yogic koshas or subtle bodies. That's one of the reasons this can seem rather dull. The stories that this cuts through are so much more colourful and fascinating.

If we'd come together this afternoon to study the chakric system, think how much more we would be able to say, just about that one aspect of spiritual psycho-philosophy. We could have such fun with the chakras. We could sit here and clear our chakric blocks with visualisations. We could visualise a different crystal in each chakra, a different colour, a different symbol, a different sound, a different quality. We could visualise a blue sapphire pyramid and chant 'Aum' in the vishuddha chakra to develop the quality of truthfulness. We could give each other auric massages. This is what the mind does. It makes up such lovely stories.

Run away from non-duality because compared to the chakras and the koshas, this is dull. But remember that as long as we are fascinated by all these other stories, we're missing the fascination of this. While we're focussing on developing compassion in our heart by meditating on the rose quartz orb of love in the anahata chakra, we're missing the miracle of this, the miracle of the ivy climbing up the wall outside the window.

I could suggest that liberation is simply a loss, that there's nothing to be gained from it. Or I could suggest that seeing the ivy climbing up the wall as a miracle is some compensation.

Do we come to these meetings to be reminded of our true nature? Even when the message is clear, we still want to come. I don't know why I came here today but there is something that makes me make the effort. What is it that draws me here despite having understood intellectually a good part of it, despite having already heard it repeatedly?

Your question may be about personal motivation, in which case there could be many different answers. There may be a sense that though you have understood a good deal of this conceptually, that's not actually relevant if there's still a feeling of separation. But the answer that I prefer is that occasionally, for no reason at all, Oneness delights in hearing itself spoken about as clearly as possible. Most of the time Oneness prefers to watch Arsenal play Manchester United or to get drunk or to save the planet or to buy a new hat. But occasionally Oneness gives rise to a scene in the play called 'Oneness Delights In Listening To Itself Talking About Itself As Clearly As Possible'. I prefer that to any other answer because it takes purpose out of it.

I remember being at one of your talks where you introduced it by saying that it was purposeless.

Yes it is purposeless. But so is everything else. Let's be clear about this, I can definitely confirm that you are wasting your time here. But of course you are also wasting your time anywhere else. In addition there's no you and no time which you could waste. So it doesn't matter. You might as well be here as anywhere else, but there's no choice about that. There is no possibility that this could be different to what it is.

And there's a possibility that Oneness delights in listening to itself?

That's not a possibility. It's definite.

This Oneness is really narcissistic, isn't it. (Laughter)

That may be personalising Oneness a bit too much. But Oneness is everything, including narcissism.

⁑⁑⁑⁑⁑⁑⁑⁑⁑

Is it our identification with pain that actually makes it seem worse?

Toothache is toothache.

But in the ordinary separated state, isn't it the sense that it's 'me' that's got the toothache that makes it worse?

There are certain kinds of suffering which arise directly from the existence of a person, particularly a neurotic person. So we could suggest that these forms of suffering might arise less or die away if the person has been seen through. That's the good news. But the bad news is that the person, particularly the neurotic person, is also very good at attenuating suffering, at filtering it out. The person is very good at erecting barriers to suffering and turning down its volume. If the person isn't there doing that anymore, the volume of the suffering could increase. Neurotic feelings might decrease but natural feelings might get stronger. Natural feelings are often more powerful than neurotic feelings although they don't tend to last as long.

If there were anybody who could do anything about it, you might make your own calculation about the trade-off. Is it better to have two days of irritation or five minutes of anger? If you'd prefer the five minutes of anger, go for liberation. If you'd prefer the two days of irritation, stick with neurosis. Of course this is all nonsense because there's nobody who can go for either. But it has been noticed here and in talking to others that the filters can come off when liberation is seen, so feelings might become more powerful, including those feelings that we label 'uncomfortable'.

What about the toothache itself?

Toothache is toothache. Go to the dentist. Take analgesics. This doesn't make any difference.

Sometimes, particularly if there's been an exposure to the stories of spiritual paths, this kind of question arises from the belief that there must be a blessed state which can be attained which is beyond any possibility of pain and suffering.

And if the analgesics don't work?

The answer doesn't become any different. As I said before, phenomena don't change.

Leaving psychological baggage aside, pain alone can condition the mind in many ways.

It can appear to condition the mind. There may be a scene in the play which is scripted that way. That's a terribly misleading phrase because it implies that there's a script-writer, which of course there isn't. Nevertheless, if there are scenes in the play in which

John has a lot of pain, that's likely to contribute a different script to John's mental processes. That's how things are in the world of phenomena.

Many of the stories about pain add meaning to it. It's easy to understand how this can happen. It's the mind's compensation for living a difficult life. Many of the stories suggest in different ways that pain is somehow good for us. "There's no gain without pain." "Pain strengthens the spirit." "Pain purifies the soul." We invent many stories about pain. It's an obvious thing for a person to do. We often tell these stories to give comfort to ourselves and to other people because at times life can seem very difficult for a person.

These stories are all balderdash.

Yes, but we can understand why the person invents them. It's difficult for a person to be living in a state of separation in any case. If there are further difficulties like pain, or problems with relationships, or bankruptcy, it's not surprising that we invent stories to comfort ourselves that it is meaningful or that it is good for us. This is why we can be left feeling so desperate if the sense of meaning leaves but the sense of a person remains. If the person has been sustained throughout their suffering by a sense of faith and then their faith disappears, they may find themselves in the dark night of the soul.

I was just thinking of a connection between what you said about all religions and spiritual paths seeming to offer a permanent state of peace and how having a sense of separation is difficult enough in itself.

It's the root of all difficulties.

And on top of that we've got all the other problems, so is it any wonder that we want this permanent state of peace? It's based on our experience of real difficulties throughout our lives, to put it mildly.

We can become desperate in the story. At an extreme we may join a suicide cult and drink the cyanide as we wait for the alien spaceship to arrive to take us to another dimension.

For a person who has no possible way of seeing that they are not a person, attaining a permanent state of bliss can seem like the way out. The way out of suffering may seem to be for us to attain a state where we do not suffer. How can it possibly be understood that the way out of personal suffering is to see that there is no 'me' who suffers?

But that doesn't mean an end to toothache as long as there are teeth.

****

Can I get back to the question of time again? There can only be a sense of the passage of time because there is something that doesn't move, a stillness. I'm just wondering whether from your experience ...

It's not from my experience.

O.k. But it seems to me that there can only be knowledge of the passing of events because somewhere there's the knowing of a still-ness against which these passing events are contrasted. Could that be said to be the void?

For a person there may only be the passing of time. There may not be the seeing of stillness, or the void. But where stillness is seen, what you say makes perfect sense. There is the seeing of absolute silence, absolute stillness, from which all sound and all movement arises. Stillness is seen, silence is heard, but not by me, not by you, not by any person.

It is movement and sound which creates the sense of time.

No one sees it and nothing is seen and yet the statement "stillness is known" still means something.

231

I prefer 'Stillness is seen' because 'known' has connotations of an idea, a thought. Stillness and silence cannot be known conceptually. However, they can be seen. When they are seen, this cuts through any idea of stilling the mind. The idea that I have to still my mind can seem so persuasive. It arises out of a misunderstanding of the communication that this is about stillness and silence. The mind gets hold of that communication and says "Aha! This is about stillness and silence. I, the mind, am restless and noisy so I must make myself still and silent." Out of that idea come techniques whereby the mind tries to do this as an activity.

This is exactly the wrong way round. If liberation is seen, then stillness is seen. But we can't get ourselves to see liberation by making ourselves still. Stillness and silence have nothing to do with stopping thought, or with making the mind quiet or inactive. When stillness is seen, thoughts do not interrupt it. Thoughts are stillness arising as thoughts.

Seeing liberation is impersonal. It has nothing to do with the personal mind or with the activity it may engage or not engage in.

You are saying that personal endeavour just gets in the way?

Nothing can get in the way. I'm simply saying that personal endeavour is irrelevant. But if you go to see a teacher and take on the concept that you should be sitting here quietening the mind and not having any thoughts, then that's probably what you'll be doing.

So is anything I try to do to see this a waste of time?

Like what? Purifying your chakras? Being good? Both? Yes, it's a waste of time, but of course so is everything else, so it's fine.

I don't want us to start evolving a method here, although if we did I could put the prices up. It would become a more expensive way of wasting time, but still cheaper than some others like becoming an alcoholic.

Anything we do is simply irrelevant. As there's no 'we' who's doing it, there's no possibility that it could be otherwise.

People often ask "What's the point of coming here?" It's better to take a step back from that question and recognise that there was never any possibility of this being any different. So we can forget about motivation or questions like "Should I have come here? Would I be better off somewhere else? Should I spend my money on going to India to see a guru or having an aura massage?" These questions are irrelevant because there is never any possibility that anything can be other than what it is. In a sense you could say these questions have no meaning because they are about an illusion.

In the same way, I might have had a dream last night in which I was standing at a railway station buying a ticket to Birmingham. There would be no point in my sitting here now wondering if I should have gone to Brighton instead. It was a dream. It couldn't have been any different and nothing actually happened.

It's the same with real life?

That's the point I'm trying to make. In 'real life' you are standing at a railway station apparently making a decision about your destination and it has no more reality and no more meaning than it does in your night-time dream.

We add on the meaning and that can be self-torture. "Should I have done this rather than that?"

There might be the possibility of an 'Aha!' and some relaxation if we take a step back from these questions and recognise even conceptually that they are all irrelevant because there is never any possibility that anything could be different to what it is. This is of course a very obvious statement to make. But because of the illusion of time it's not necessarily easy for us to realise this. We might think "It's all very well for him to say that, but I know there is a past and in that past I could have made a different decision." No, there isn't a past. There is always only this in which nothing could possibly be any different to what it is.

I don't know how many molecules of H_2O there are in this

glass of water, but there is no possibility of there being one more or one less than there is.

You're saying that what exists, exists?

Yes, I'm saying something as obvious as that. If we could really get that, even conceptually, it might produce some relaxation. Remember, if there were a method, it might be 'Relax.'

I'm going to ask you to repeat that.

Are you listening carefully? Relax.

****

Is stillness and silence a necessary precursor to awakening? There might not be anything we can do, but when you were at Charing Cross Station you weren't actually in a state of perturbation at the time? In the mind and experience of Richard there was silence?

No. There was no Richard's experience, there was no mind, there was simply Charing Cross Station happening.

I was thinking of the second before that, actually.

I was reading the evening newspaper. Do you want to know which page?

I would have thought that there was a peaceful state in the moments before awakening.

No. Forget it. You're looking for another cause and effect or technique. "If I can get into a state of peace sitting on this train recognising that life is beautiful, that may be helpful." No. There's no cause and effect. Nothing causes the dropping away of the person, not even reading the evening newspaper.

What about the thirty years of meditation?

There was no thirty years of meditation. No one meditated. That's the shock when this is seen. That's the realisation. This has nothing to do with anything I thought I was or anything I thought I had done. There is no one who needs to be purified so that they can become holy enough to receive liberation.

(Laughing) This is a terrible message! It's just awful! There's nothing to be done. Spiritual paths and religions arise out of a sense of inadequacy. "I am not yet holy enough to become enlightened or to be taken into heaven or to experience bliss." People feel this because of their sense of separation. We know we've lost something. In addition, if we've been brought up in a Christian culture we keep being told that it's our fault that we've lost it. At the age of five we might go to school or to church and be faced with the symbol of a man nailed to a cross. Then we might be told "That's your fault! You did that!" We could reply "But I'm only five." "Nevertheless," they say, "it's your fault because of original sin!" So many things shout at us "You'd better do something about yourself. It's up to you to do something about it."

You are not inadequate. How could you be inadequate? You are Oneness being John or Mary or Timothy. How could Oneness possibly be inadequate? You are already the divine expression.

But the mind wants to set itself a task. What could be a more noble task than to purify ourself, to make ourself ready to be raised up into heaven or to become enlightened? It's a great way of passing time, a very meaningful way. It's so much more noble than shopping or becoming an alcoholic. But there's no one who needs purifying, there's no one who needs to become more adequate. I am the divine expression and so are you and so is this carpet.

If we're used to structuring our time through a religious path or spiritual practices, seeing liberation can create a bit of a problem.

Why?

Because if we really get this, or rather if it is really got, we may lose our way of structuring time. We may need to find something else to do between morning and night. I recommend going to the park and looking at trees and squirrels but that doesn't suit everybody.

There's a brief Oriental poem:

How can we ever lose interest in life?
Spring has come again
And cherry trees bloom on the mountains.

I feel that must have been written by somebody who wasn't there. When there's somebody there, cherry trees blooming on the mountains are often not enough. We usually need stocks and shares and Mercedes and military coups, things like that, to make life interesting.

The ordinary things in life like cherry blossom can seem very precious when someone is dying.

I was talking to a friend recently whose partner died last year. She gave a magical description of their last three months together. All the seeking and striving and 'futuring' became irrelevant and what was left was just the enjoyment of presence, of 'the moment'.

Phenomena don't change. The squirrel on the tree trunk doesn't become bigger or change colour. But it may be perceived that this is a miracle arising out of nothing, a complete mystery.

When we stop telling ourselves stories about meaning in our head, this may be seen for what it is and it may be seen as sufficient. Then it doesn't need any added excitement. It's seen through the eyes of a child again.

Why do we need separateness?

We don't need it. It just happens.

In a spiritual school that I studied in, it was said that in the

Garden of Eden, original sin was the knowing of duality, the knowing of self-consciousness.

That's how that story makes most sense. The fruit of the tree of knowledge is self-consciousness. "They saw each other and they *knew* that they were naked."

What would the serpent be?

The serpent is the catalyst. The serpent is their greatest friend. The serpent allows them to break away from slavish unselfconscious obedience.

Where does evil come into it?

Where would you like evil to come into it?

What is evil? What does it consist of?

It's whatever story you want it to be. As I've already said, the mind is so constructed as to look for binary opposites in order to produce a story with meaning – God and Satan, good and evil. As soon as we have good and evil we have structured our time between birth and death very successfully, because now we can fight evil and uphold good by, for example, slaughtering the heathen. Meanwhile the heathen can uphold good and fight evil by slaughtering us. It's a perfect symbiotic relationship, a symphony of warfare.

If we want to be more sophisticated about it and look at it psychologically because we're now in the twenty-first century, we could say that evil is a projection of the shadow. That's a much more intelligent way of looking at it and within the story it's a much more useful way of looking at it because it's less likely to lead to the killing of heathens.

Evil is the shadow projected. You could say that when the shadow is integrated, there is no evil and we stop setting fire to our own houses and our neighbours' houses, to use Jung's wonderful metaphor.

237

How is the shadow integrated?

We're really getting into a psychological story now. I'm reluctant to end the afternoon on such a note but as we've started, let's go on. To answer the question, firstly the shadow is recognised and secondly it is owned. That's it. It's very simple. "He who bears his own shadow liberates the collective." In other words, each person who recognises and owns his own shadow helps the commonality of people to recognise and own their own shadow too. When that happens, the shadow is no longer projected and then we no longer see others as evil. We no longer interpret 'out there' as evil.

(Laughing) That's a terrible note to end the afternoon on. I want every one of you sitting here to take an oath of secrecy so that you will not go out there and say "He was supposed to be talking about non-duality but he ended up talking about Jung and owning the shadow." Otherwise I'll be excommunicated by the Convocation of Non-Duality Bishops.

But if we're going to tell a story, that's a wonderful one to tell. I'd much rather go into the story told by Jung than the story told by The Plymouth Brethren. It's much more intelligent and it makes much more sense.

12
Postscript

This sounds like a blessing for nobody.

That's a great line to end on.

References

P.xii "Everything that comes from birth undoes itself in liberation"
Jen Smith

P.10 "I have given suck, and know
     How tender 'tis to love the babe that milks me."
William Shakespeare – *Macbeth*.

P.11 "The world is everything that is the case."
Ludwig Wittgenstein – *Tractatus Logico-Philosophicus*.
London: Routledge, 2001

P.43 "I tell you, we are here on Earth to fart around and don't let anybody tell you different."
Kurt Vonnegut – *Timequake*.
Jonathan Cape: London, 1997

P.44 "Even in the greatest yogi, sorrow and joy still arise just as before."
Dudjom Rinpoche.

P.49 "Nothing worth reading has been written about it."
Stuart Sutherland in *The International Dictionary of Psychology*.
New York: The Crossroad Publishing Company, 1989

P.48 "Psychology is not ready to tackle the issue of consciouness."
Ulric Neisser quoted by Amit Goswami in *The Self-Aware Universe*.
New York: Jeremy P. Tarcher, 1995

P.72 "It's a tale ...... full of sound and fury, signifying nothing."
William Shakespeare – *Macbeth*.

P.76 "Love Dreams Differences Where There Are None."
Terry Murphy.

P.77 "Everything ends in mystery."
Heraclitus.

P.88 "Except you become as little children you will not enter the Kingdom of Heaven."
The Gospel According to Matthew.

P.93 "O body swayed to music, O brightening glance,
    How can we know the dancer from the dance?"
W.B. Yeats – *Among School Children – Collected Poems.*
New York: Scribner, 1996

P.95 "You can say 'Gee, your life must be pretty bleak if you don't think there's a purpose.' But I'm anticipating having a good lunch."
James Watson quoted by Richard Dawkins in *The God Delusion.*
Boston: Mariner Books, 2008

P.97
"Just rest.
For you separation from God,
From love,
Is the hardest work
In this world.
You can use my soft words
As a cushion
For your
Head."
Hafiz – *The Gift.*

P.121 "Now this soul has fallen from love into nothingness, and without such nothingness she cannot be All."
Marguerite Porete quoted by John Dourley in *Jung and the Mystical Experience of Nothingness.*
London: The Guild Of Pastoral Psychology; Lecture No. 289, 2006

P.132 "You may feel the need to become more aware, be here now, enter the stillness ..."
Nathan Gill – *Clarity.*
Salisbury: Non-Duality Press, 2005

P.152 "If then I bend over and pick up a stick, he is instantly before me ..."
Allen Wheelis – *The Listener. A Psychoanalyst Examines His Life.*
New York: W. W. Norton & Co., 1999

241

P.162 "I'd like to help you but unfortunately in Zen we don't have anything."
Ikkyu quoted by Timothy Freke in *The Wisdom of Zen Masters*.
Newton Abbot: David Charles, 1999

P.162 "You must be aware that this training may not give you any result whatsoever."
Janwillem van de Wetering – *A Glimpse of Nothingness*.
New York: St. Martin's Press, 1999

P.177 "At death there is only liberation. It's just more chic to see liberation while you're alive."
Max Furlaud in a conversation with the author.

P.201 "Truth is a pathless land"
J. Krishnamurti – speech dissolving the Order of the Star.

P.236   "How can we ever lose interest in life?
         Spring has come again
         And cherry trees bloom on the mountains."
Ryokan.

P.237 "And the eyes of the two of them were opened and they knew that they were naked."
The Book of Genesis.

P.238 "He who bears his own shadow liberates the collective."
Sylvia Brinton Perera – *The Scapegoat Complex.*
Toronto: Inner City Books, 1985

Contact Richard Sylvester

Richard Sylvester lives in England on the border of West Kent and East Sussex. He gives talks on Non-duality and Liberation in London and other places.

Richard can be contacted by e-mailing
richardsylvester@hotmail.co.uk

To find out more visit
www.richardsylvester.com

LaVergne, TN USA
28 August 2009
156271LV00003B/150/P